Bio-Innovators Blueprint

Startup Ideas in Biotechnology

Ramatenki Saye Ddarshanu

Copyright and Credits

Credits:

Author: Ramatenki Saye Ddarshanu

The information and insights presented in this book have been created solely by [Your Name], the author, in collaboration with OpenAI's GPT-3.5 language model. As an AI language model, GPT-3.5 provided general information and knowledge up to its knowledge cutoff in September 2021. The content generated by GPT-3.5 is purely informational and does not constitute professional advice or endorsement.

Disclaimer: While every effort has been made to ensure the accuracy of the information presented in this book, [Your Name] and OpenAI make no representations or warranties regarding the completeness, accuracy, reliability, or suitability of the content. The reader is responsible for evaluating the information and determining its applicability to their specific circumstances. Neither [Your Name] nor OpenAI shall be held liable for any damages arising from the use of the information contained in this book.

Acknowledgments:

I would like to express my gratitude to OpenAI for developing the remarkable GPT-3.5 language model, which has been an invaluable tool in generating the content for this book. Its capacity to assist authors and provide insights has been instrumental in shaping "Bio-Innovators' Blueprint: Startup Ideas in Biotechnology."

I would also like to extend heartfelt thanks to the teams and individuals behind OpenAI for their dedication to advancing artificial intelligence and natural language processing, pushing the boundaries of what's possible.

Last but not least, thank you to the readers of this book for embarking on this journey with me. May the knowledge and inspiration shared within these pages spark the flame of innovation in the field of biotechnology entrepreneurship.

Contents :

Chapter 1: Introduction to Biotechnology Startups

Section 1: Understanding the Biotechnology Landscape

- What is Biotechnology?

  - Defining biotechnology and its multidisciplinary nature.

  - Historical milestones and the evolution of biotech innovations.

- Biotechnology in Today's World

  - The far-reaching impact of biotech on various industries.

  - Biotechnology's role in addressing global challenges and improving human life.

- Exploring Biotech Subfields

  - Medical Biotechnology: Advancements in healthcare and therapies.

  - Agricultural Biotechnology: Innovations in crop improvement and food production.

  - Environmental Biotechnology: Solutions for a sustainable future.

Section 2: Importance of Entrepreneurship in Biotech

- The Entrepreneurial Mindset in Biotechnology

  - The characteristics of successful biotech entrepreneurs.

  - Navigating risk and uncertainty in the biotech industry.

- Biotech Startups vs. Traditional Biotech Companies

  - Advantages and challenges of launching a startup in biotechnology.

  - Creating an innovative culture within a startup environment.

Section 3: Overview of Biotech Startup Ecosystem

- Biotech Startup Lifecycle

  - Phases of a biotech startup: from ideation to commercialization.

  - Common pitfalls and best practices in each stage.

- Key Players in the Biotech Ecosystem

  - Universities and research institutions: fostering innovation.

  - Incubators, accelerators, and innovation hubs: supporting startups.

  - Investors and venture capitalists: funding breakthroughs.

- Collaborations and Partnerships

  - Industry partnerships and technology transfer agreements.

  - Building strategic alliances for growth and resource-sharing.

Section 4: Ethical Considerations in Biotech Entrepreneurship

- The Ethical Landscape of Biotechnology

  - Balancing progress and ethical boundaries in biotech ventures.

  - Ethical implications of gene editing, personalized medicine, and more.

- Responsible Innovation and Social Impact

  - Incorporating sustainability and social responsibility into startup missions.

  - Ethical frameworks for decision-making in biotech entrepreneurship.

Section 1: Understanding the Biotechnology Landscape

What is Biotechnology?

Biotechnology is a cutting-edge field that merges biology, chemistry, and technology to develop innovative solutions to address a wide array of challenges. At its core, biotechnology harnesses living organisms and their biological processes to create products and technologies that benefit society. From life-saving medical treatments to sustainable agricultural practices and environmental conservation, biotechnology has revolutionized industries across the globe.

This section introduces readers to the fundamental principles of biotechnology and its multidisciplinary nature. We explore the historical milestones that have shaped the field, from the discovery of DNA's structure to the development of breakthrough gene-editing technologies like CRISPR-Cas9. Understanding these foundational aspects of biotechnology will provide a context for the transformative potential that biotech startups hold in today's world.

Biotechnology in Today's World

The impact of biotechnology reaches far beyond the confines of laboratories. This subsection highlights how biotech innovations have transformed industries and influenced our daily lives. In

the realm of healthcare, biotechnology has enabled the development of personalized medicine, gene therapies, and diagnostic tools that were once unimaginable. The agricultural sector has benefited from genetically modified crops and advanced breeding techniques, improving food production and enhancing resilience to environmental challenges.

Furthermore, biotechnology plays a critical role in environmental preservation. By employing bioremediation, biofuels, and waste management solutions, biotech startups contribute to a greener and more sustainable future. This section also examines the intersection of biotechnology with emerging fields such as synthetic biology and digital health, showcasing the limitless possibilities for biotech entrepreneurs to shape the future.

Exploring Biotech Subfields

Biotechnology encompasses diverse subfields, each offering unique opportunities for innovation and entrepreneurship. In this subsection, we delve deeper into key areas within biotechnology:

Medical Biotechnology: Advancements in Healthcare and Therapies

Here, we focus on the breakthroughs in medical biotechnology that have revolutionized the diagnosis and treatment of diseases. We explore biopharmaceuticals, gene therapies, regenerative medicine, and the potential of personalized medicine to tailor treatments based on individual genetics and health profiles.

Agricultural Biotechnology: Innovations in Crop Improvement and Food Production

The agricultural sector faces the challenge of feeding a growing global population while minimizing environmental impacts. This subsection explores how agricultural biotechnology offers solutions through genetically modified organisms (GMOs), precision agriculture, and advancements in crop breeding techniques.

Environmental Biotechnology: Solutions for a Sustainable Future

As environmental issues become increasingly urgent, biotechnology emerges as a powerful tool to address these challenges. We examine how biotech startups contribute to environmental conservation, pollution remediation, and sustainable resource management through bio-based solutions.

By understanding the breadth and depth of these biotech subfields, aspiring entrepreneurs can gain insights into the diverse areas ripe for innovation and identify their areas of interest and expertise. In the subsequent chapters, we will explore how to translate these insights into actionable and impactful biotech startup ideas.

Section 2: Importance of Entrepreneurship in Biotech

The Entrepreneurial Mindset in Biotechnology

The success of biotechnology startups heavily relies on the entrepreneurial mindset of their founders. In this section, we explore the key attributes and characteristics that make biotech entrepreneurs stand out. We delve into the significance of creativity, resilience, and adaptability in the face of challenges that are inherent in the biotech industry. Understanding the entrepreneurial mindset will empower aspiring bio-innovators to navigate the uncertainties and complexities of biotech entrepreneurship with confidence.

Navigating Risk and Uncertainty in the Biotech Industry

Biotech startups operate in a high-risk environment due to the long development timelines, regulatory hurdles, and complex scientific challenges involved. Here, we discuss strategies to manage and mitigate risks effectively. This includes identifying potential roadblocks early on, forming contingency plans, and cultivating a culture that embraces calculated risk-taking. Furthermore, we explore how biotech entrepreneurs can leverage failure as a valuable learning experience, fostering a culture of experimentation and continuous improvement.

Biotech Startups vs. Traditional Biotech Companies

This subsection highlights the distinct advantages and challenges that biotech startups face compared to their well-established counterparts. We explore the nimbleness and agility of startups in driving innovation and responding to emerging opportunities. Conversely, we also address the resource constraints that startups encounter and how creative solutions and strategic partnerships can help overcome these challenges.

Creating an Innovative Culture within a Startup Environment

A strong entrepreneurial culture is crucial to the success of biotech startups. We examine how founders can foster an environment that encourages creativity, collaboration, and open communication among team members. Emphasizing the value of diversity and interdisciplinary collaboration, we explore how diverse perspectives and skillsets can lead to groundbreaking biotech innovations.

By understanding the importance of entrepreneurship in biotechnology and the role it plays in shaping successful biotech startups, readers will be motivated to embrace their entrepreneurial spirit. The section will inspire readers to cultivate the necessary traits and mindset to thrive as bio-innovators, providing them with the foundation they need to embark on their entrepreneurial journey in the dynamic world of biotechnology.

Section 3: Overview of Biotech Startup Ecosystem

Biotech Startup Lifecycle

This subsection provides readers with an in-depth understanding of the different phases involved in the lifecycle of a biotech startup. From the initial ideation stage, where entrepreneurs conceive innovative biotech solutions, to the commercialization and growth phases, we explore the critical milestones and challenges at each step. Understanding the startup lifecycle enables aspiring bio-innovators to navigate their journey with clarity, ensuring they have the necessary strategies and resources in place at each stage of development.

Key Players in the Biotech Ecosystem

In this section, we shed light on the essential players that form the backbone of the biotech startup ecosystem. We delve into the role of academic research institutions and universities as vital sources of innovation and potential collaborators for startups. Readers will also gain insights into the support and resources offered by incubators, accelerators, and innovation hubs specifically tailored to biotech startups. Moreover, we explore the importance of investors and venture capitalists in providing critical funding and expertise to help biotech startups scale and thrive.

Collaborations and Partnerships

Strategic collaborations and partnerships play a pivotal role in the success of biotech startups. This subsection explores the different forms of collaborations that startups can engage in, from research partnerships with academic institutions to industry partnerships with established biotech companies. We discuss the benefits of collaborating with other startups and sharing resources for mutual growth. Additionally, we highlight the significance of technology transfer agreements and licensing deals in maximizing the value of a startup's intellectual property.

Understanding the intricacies of the biotech startup ecosystem equips readers with the knowledge to navigate this complex landscape successfully. By recognizing the key players and potential collaborators, aspiring biotech entrepreneurs can build a network of support and resources to fuel their startup's growth and development. As they progress through the chapters, they will learn how to leverage these connections and partnerships to propel their biotech startup towards success.

Section 4: Ethical Considerations in Biotech Entrepreneurship

Ethics is a crucial aspect of biotechnology entrepreneurship, given the profound impact that biotech innovations can have on individuals, societies, and the environment. In this section, we delve into the complex ethical considerations that arise in the realm of biotech startups, and we explore how responsible innovation can drive positive change.

The Ethical Landscape of Biotechnology

Biotechnology presents unique ethical challenges due to its potential to manipulate life at the molecular level. We examine the ethical dilemmas associated with gene editing technologies, such as CRISPR-Cas9, which have the power to modify the human genome. Additionally, we discuss the ethical implications of personalized medicine, where decisions about individuals' health and treatment are based on genetic information.

Responsible Innovation and Social Impact

Responsible innovation involves carefully considering the potential risks and consequences of biotech advancements while maximizing their positive impact. This subsection highlights the importance of social impact assessments to ensure that biotech startups' innovations are aligned with societal values and needs. By emphasizing the incorporation of ethical considerations from the early stages of product development, readers will understand the significance of building a sustainable and socially responsible biotech venture.

Examples of Ethical Dilemmas and Solutions

To illustrate the ethical challenges faced by biotech entrepreneurs, we present real-world examples of biotech startups that have encountered ethical dilemmas and how they navigated them responsibly. For instance, we examine a startup working on a groundbreaking gene-editing therapy for a rare genetic disease. We explore the considerations they faced regarding consent, accessibility, and the potential implications of editing the germline. By studying these cases, readers will gain insights into the complexities of ethical decision-making and the need to strike a balance between innovation and ethical responsibility.

Frameworks for Ethical Decision-Making

To guide biotech entrepreneurs in making ethical decisions, we present various ethical frameworks commonly used in bioethics. These frameworks, such as the principles of beneficence, non-maleficence, autonomy, and justice, serve as valuable tools to evaluate the ethical implications of biotech innovations. Readers will learn how to apply these principles to their own startup endeavors, ensuring that their products and technologies align with ethical guidelines and promote the greater good.

By exploring the ethical considerations in biotech entrepreneurship and understanding the importance of responsible innovation, readers will be empowered to develop startups that not only drive scientific progress but also uphold ethical standards and societal values. As they embark on their bio-innovator journey, they will recognize the significance of ethical responsibility in shaping a positive and sustainable future through biotechnology.

Chapter 2: Exploring Biotechnology Trends

Gene Editing and Genetic Engineering :

Gene Editing and Genetic Engineering have emerged as groundbreaking technologies in the field of biotechnology, enabling scientists to manipulate the genetic information of organisms with remarkable precision. Here, we delve deeper into this trend and explore notable examples of gene editing and genetic engineering in various sectors:

1. Medical Breakthroughs: CRISPR Therapies

One of the most prominent examples of gene editing in the medical field is the development of CRISPR-based therapies. CRISPR-Cas9, a revolutionary gene-editing tool, allows scientists to target specific genes and make precise modifications. Biotech startups are leveraging this technology to develop potential cures for genetic diseases. For instance, researchers have used CRISPR to correct mutations responsible for diseases like cystic fibrosis, sickle cell anemia, and muscular dystrophy in laboratory models. These breakthroughs hold the promise of providing life-changing treatments for patients with genetic disorders.

2. Agriculture: Genetically Modified Crops

Genetic engineering has transformed agriculture by creating genetically modified (GM) crops with enhanced traits. Biotech startups have developed GM crops that are resistant to pests, diseases, and environmental stresses. For example, startups have engineered crops with improved drought tolerance, ensuring greater resilience in the face of climate change. Additionally, GM crops with enhanced nutritional profiles offer potential solutions to address malnutrition and improve food security in vulnerable populations.

3. Industrial Biotechnology: Biofuel Production

Gene editing and genetic engineering have revolutionized industrial biotechnology, particularly in the production of biofuels. Startups are engineering microorganisms like algae and bacteria to efficiently convert renewable feedstocks, such as plant biomass and waste materials, into biofuels like bioethanol and biodiesel. These advancements reduce greenhouse gas emissions, provide renewable energy alternatives, and contribute to sustainable transportation solutions.

4. Therapeutic Applications: CAR-T Cell Therapy

In the realm of healthcare, gene editing has paved the way for novel therapeutic approaches like CAR-T cell therapy. Startups are using gene editing techniques to modify a patient's immune cells, enhancing their ability to target and destroy cancer cells. CAR-T cell therapies have demonstrated remarkable success in treating certain types of leukemia and lymphoma, offering new hope to patients who previously had limited treatment options.

5. Disease-Resistant Livestock

Genetic engineering holds the potential to improve livestock health and well-being. Biotech startups are exploring ways to develop disease-resistant livestock by modifying genes associated with susceptibility to specific diseases. For instance, researchers have explored gene editing in pigs to create animals resistant to African Swine Fever, a devastating viral disease that affects the swine industry.

These examples represent just a fraction of the vast possibilities that gene editing and genetic engineering offer. The potential for transformative applications in medicine, agriculture, industry, and beyond continues to expand as biotech startups push the boundaries of innovation. Aspiring bio-innovators can draw inspiration from these examples and consider how they, too, can leverage gene editing and genetic engineering to address pressing challenges and make a positive impact on the world.

Personalized Medicine and Precision Therapies

Personalized Medicine and Precision Therapies have emerged as a revolutionary approach to healthcare, tailoring medical treatments to an individual's unique genetic makeup, lifestyle, and environment. This personalized approach offers the potential to enhance treatment outcomes, minimize side effects, and optimize patient care. Here, we explore the growing significance of personalized medicine and precision therapies, along with notable examples in various medical fields:

1. Pharmacogenomics: Optimizing Drug Response

Pharmacogenomics is a key component of personalized medicine, where genetic information is used to predict an individual's response to specific medications. Biotech startups are developing genetic tests that analyze a patient's DNA to identify variations that influence drug metabolism and efficacy. This information helps physicians prescribe medications that are most likely to work effectively for each patient while reducing the risk of adverse reactions. For instance, patients with certain genetic variants may require different dosages of a medication, and pharmacogenomics allows healthcare providers to customize treatment regimens accordingly.

2. Cancer Immunotherapy: CAR-T Cell Therapy

Precision therapies are revolutionizing cancer treatment, particularly with CAR-T cell therapy. This personalized immunotherapy involves genetically modifying a patient's own immune cells, called T cells, to recognize and attack cancer cells. Biotech startups are at the forefront of this cutting-edge therapy, engineering T cells to express chimeric antigen receptors (CARs) that target specific cancer antigens. Notable success stories include the FDA approval of CAR-T cell therapies for certain types of leukemia and lymphoma, where patients achieved remission after other treatments had failed.

3. Companion Diagnostics: Tailoring Treatments

Companion diagnostics play a pivotal role in personalized medicine by matching patients with the most suitable treatments based on genetic testing results. Biotech startups are developing companion diagnostic tests that identify specific biomarkers associated with diseases, helping physicians select the most effective therapies for individual patients. For example, a companion diagnostic test can determine if a patient's tumor expresses a particular protein, making them eligible for a targeted therapy that specifically addresses that protein's activity.

4. Preventive Medicine: Genetic Risk Assessments

Personalized medicine extends to preventive care, where genetic risk assessments empower individuals to make informed lifestyle choices. Biotech startups are offering genetic tests that assess an individual's predisposition to certain diseases, such as heart disease, diabetes, and certain cancers. Armed with this information, patients can adopt tailored preventive measures, such as lifestyle changes or increased surveillance, to reduce their risk of developing certain conditions.

5. Infectious Disease Management: Precision Antimicrobial Therapy

Infectious disease management benefits from precision approaches to antimicrobial therapy. Biotech startups are using genomic data from pathogens to guide the selection of the most appropriate antibiotics for patients with infections. This personalized approach helps combat antibiotic resistance by optimizing antibiotic use and avoiding unnecessary treatments.

These examples highlight the transformative impact of personalized medicine and precision therapies in various aspects of healthcare. As biotech startups continue to advance these innovative approaches, the future of medicine looks increasingly promising, with the potential to revolutionize patient care and outcomes. The integration of genomic information, advanced technologies, and data-driven approaches will continue to drive the evolution of personalized medicine, making it an integral part of modern healthcare.

Synthetic Biology and Bioengineering

Synthetic Biology and Bioengineering represent a cutting-edge field within biotechnology that involves designing and constructing artificial biological systems to create novel functionalities and applications. These innovative approaches have far-reaching implications across various industries, ranging from healthcare and agriculture to environmental sustainability and industrial production. Here, we explore the significance of Synthetic Biology and Bioengineering, along with notable examples of their applications:

1. Industrial Biotechnology: Bio-Based Materials

Biotech startups are harnessing Synthetic Biology and Bioengineering to develop bio-based materials as sustainable alternatives to conventional products. For example, startups are engineering microorganisms to produce bio-plastics that are biodegradable and environmentally friendly. These bio-plastics have the potential to replace traditional plastics derived from fossil fuels, reducing plastic waste and its impact on the environment.

2. Pharmaceutical Production: Recombinant Proteins

Synthetic Biology enables the production of complex proteins with therapeutic potential. Biotech startups use genetically engineered microorganisms to produce recombinant proteins, such as insulin, growth factors, and antibodies. These proteins are crucial components in advanced medical therapies, diagnostics, and biopharmaceutical drugs. By using synthetic biology techniques, startups can efficiently produce large quantities of these valuable proteins at lower costs compared to traditional methods.

3. Bioenergy: Microbial Fuel Cells

Bioengineering plays a significant role in the development of bioenergy solutions. Biotech startups are engineering microbial fuel cells that use bacteria to convert organic matter directly into electricity. This technology holds potential for generating renewable energy from organic waste, such as agricultural residues and wastewater. Additionally, startups are exploring the use of synthetic biology to enhance the efficiency of microorganisms involved in biofuel production, such as algae-based biofuels.

4. Agricultural Biotechnology: Precision Crop Improvement

In agricultural biotechnology, Synthetic Biology and Bioengineering are being applied to develop precision crop improvement techniques. Startups are engineering plants to have specific traits, such as improved nutritional content, disease resistance, and enhanced stress tolerance. For instance, using gene editing tools, startups can develop crops with increased yields, reduced dependence on agrochemicals, and optimized nutritional profiles to address global food security challenges.

5. Environmental Remediation: Bioremediation

Synthetic Biology is employed to develop microorganisms capable of remediating environmental pollutants. Biotech startups engineer bacteria to break down hazardous contaminants in soil and water, a process known as bioremediation. By enhancing the biodegradation capabilities of these microorganisms, startups offer sustainable solutions to clean up polluted sites and restore ecosystems.

These examples demonstrate the diverse applications of Synthetic Biology and Bioengineering, showcasing the potential for innovation in various sectors. Biotech startups continue to push the boundaries of this field, harnessing the power of genetic engineering and artificial biology to create transformative solutions for pressing global challenges. As the technology advances, the impact of Synthetic Biology and Bioengineering on industries ranging from healthcare to environmental conservation is expected to grow exponentially, offering novel and sustainable approaches to address complex problems in the modern world.

Digital Health and Biomedical Technologies

Digital Health and Biomedical Technologies have ushered in a new era of healthcare, revolutionizing the way medical services are delivered, monitored, and accessed. These technologies leverage digital tools, mobile applications, wearable devices, and data analytics to empower individuals and healthcare providers with real-time information, personalized insights, and improved patient outcomes. Here, we delve deeper into the significance of Digital Health and Biomedical Technologies, along with notable examples of their applications:

1. Wearable Health Monitors

Digital health startups are developing wearable devices that continuously track vital signs and health parameters. For instance, smartwatches equipped with heart rate monitors and activity trackers empower users to monitor their physical activity, sleep patterns, and stress levels. These devices also detect irregular heart rhythms, alerting users to potential heart health issues and encouraging timely medical intervention.

2. Remote Patient Monitoring

Digital health technologies enable remote patient monitoring, a critical component of telemedicine. Startups are creating remote monitoring solutions that allow healthcare providers to track patients' health conditions from a distance. This is particularly valuable for managing chronic conditions, such as diabetes, hypertension, and respiratory diseases. Patients can upload their health data, including blood glucose levels, blood pressure readings, and oxygen saturation, enabling healthcare professionals to make timely adjustments to treatment plans and offer virtual consultations.

3. Mobile Health Applications (mHealth Apps)

mHealth apps have become increasingly popular, offering a wide range of health-related services and resources. Startups are developing mobile apps for medication reminders, mental health support, fitness coaching, and diet tracking. Some apps use machine learning algorithms to provide personalized health recommendations based on users' health data and behavior patterns.

4. Artificial Intelligence (AI) in Medical Diagnostics

Digital health startups are harnessing the power of AI and machine learning to improve medical diagnostics. AI algorithms can analyze medical images, such as X-rays and MRI scans, to assist healthcare providers in detecting diseases like cancer and identifying abnormalities. These technologies help in early detection, accurate diagnosis, and timely intervention, improving patient outcomes and reducing healthcare costs.

5. Virtual Reality (VR) in Pain Management and Rehabilitation

Virtual Reality (VR) is finding applications in pain management and rehabilitation. Digital health startups are creating VR experiences that distract patients from pain during medical procedures or aid in physiotherapy sessions for patients recovering from injuries or surgeries. VR technology can create immersive environments that engage patients' senses, easing discomfort and promoting better recovery outcomes.

6. Telemedicine Platforms

Telemedicine platforms are transforming healthcare delivery, providing remote access to medical consultations and services. Digital health startups are creating user-friendly platforms that facilitate video consultations between patients and healthcare providers. These platforms improve healthcare access, particularly in remote or underserved areas, and offer convenience to patients with mobility challenges.

These examples illustrate the transformative impact of Digital Health and Biomedical Technologies on the healthcare landscape. Biotech startups continue to innovate and integrate these technologies to enhance patient care, improve medical diagnostics, and empower individuals to take charge of their health and well-being. As these technologies advance, they have the potential to reshape the future of healthcare, making it more personalized, efficient, and accessible to people worldwide.

Environmental Biotechnology and Sustainability

Environmental Biotechnology and Sustainability focus on using biotechnological solutions to address environmental challenges and promote sustainable practices. These innovative approaches leverage biological processes and microorganisms to remediate pollution, produce eco-friendly materials, and contribute to a greener and more sustainable future. Here, we explore the significance of Environmental Biotechnology and Sustainability, along with notable examples of their applications:

1. Bioremediation: Cleaning Up Polluted Sites

Environmental Biotechnology plays a critical role in bioremediation, where microorganisms are harnessed to break down hazardous contaminants in soil and water. Biotech startups are developing specialized bacteria and fungi that can degrade pollutants, such as oil spills, heavy metals, and industrial chemicals. These environmentally friendly approaches offer sustainable solutions for cleaning up contaminated sites and restoring ecosystems.

2. Bio-based Materials: Green Alternatives

Biotech startups are engineering microorganisms to produce bio-based materials as eco-friendly alternatives to traditional products. For example, startups are using fermentation processes to produce bio-based plastics that are biodegradable and reduce plastic waste in the environment. Additionally, startups are developing bio-based textiles and building materials, offering sustainable alternatives to resource-intensive materials.

3. Waste Management: Biodegradation and Recycling

Environmental Biotechnology contributes to waste management by harnessing microorganisms to break down organic waste and convert it into useful products. Startups are working on innovative ways to use bacteria and fungi to biodegrade organic waste, reducing the burden on landfills and minimizing greenhouse gas emissions. Furthermore, biotech ventures are exploring the use of microbial processes to recycle plastics and other materials, contributing to a circular economy and reducing environmental pollution.

4. Environmental Sensors and Monitoring

Environmental Biotechnology intersects with digital technologies to develop environmental sensors and monitoring systems. Biotech startups are designing biosensors that use living organisms or biological components to detect environmental pollutants and monitor ecosystem health. These real-time monitoring systems provide valuable data to researchers, policymakers, and industries, enabling timely interventions and informed decision-making for environmental conservation.

5. Renewable Energy: Biofuels and Biogas

Environmental Biotechnology contributes to the development of renewable energy solutions, such as biofuels and biogas. Startups are engineering microorganisms to efficiently convert organic matter, agricultural residues, and waste into biofuels like bioethanol and biodiesel. Biogas production from organic waste is also gaining traction as a sustainable energy source. These renewable energy alternatives reduce greenhouse gas emissions and help transition towards a low-carbon future.

6. Sustainable Agriculture: Biofertilizers and Biological Pest Control

Biotechnology plays a role in sustainable agriculture through the development of biofertilizers and biological pest control methods. Startups are engineering beneficial microorganisms that enhance nutrient availability in soils and promote plant growth, reducing the need for synthetic fertilizers. Additionally, biotech ventures are developing biological agents to control pests and diseases, providing eco-friendly alternatives to chemical pesticides.

These examples illustrate the diverse and impactful applications of Environmental Biotechnology and Sustainability. Biotech startups continue to push the boundaries of innovation, using biotechnological solutions to address pressing environmental challenges and create a more sustainable world. As the field advances, the integration of biotechnology with environmental conservation efforts is expected to play a crucial role in fostering a greener, healthier, and more resilient planet.

Market Research and Validation

In this Chapter of "Bio-Innovators' Blueprint: Startup Ideas in Biotechnology," we dive into the crucial process of market research and validation. This chapter focuses on understanding the target market, assessing the demand for biotech innovations, and validating startup ideas to ensure they align with market needs and opportunities. Through comprehensive market research and validation, aspiring bio-innovators can build a solid foundation for their biotech startups, increasing the likelihood of success and impact.

Understanding the Target Market

The chapter begins by emphasizing the importance of identifying the target market for a biotech startup's product or service. This includes understanding the demographics, characteristics, and needs of the potential customers or end-users. For instance, if the startup is developing a new medical device, it is essential to research the specific patient populations that would benefit from the technology, as well as the preferences and requirements of healthcare professionals who might use or prescribe the device.

Market Analysis: Identifying Opportunities and Challenges

To identify market opportunities, the chapter explores methods of conducting a comprehensive market analysis. This involves examining industry trends, competitor landscape, regulatory environment, and potential barriers to entry. For example, if the biotech startup aims to introduce a novel agricultural biotechnology solution, it is crucial to analyze the existing market players, government policies, and farmer adoption rates to gauge the potential for market penetration.

Validating Startup Ideas: Proof of Concept

In this section, we discuss the importance of validating startup ideas through proof of concept studies or pilot projects. Biotech startups can conduct preliminary experiments or small-scale trials to demonstrate the feasibility and effectiveness of their innovations. For instance, a startup working on a gene therapy for a specific genetic disorder might conduct preclinical studies in animal models to validate the therapeutic concept before moving to clinical trials.

Market Research Methods and Tools

The chapter explores various market research methods and tools that biotech startups can employ to gather valuable insights. These methods may include surveys, focus groups, interviews, and data analytics. Startups can leverage digital tools and data-driven approaches to analyze market trends and customer preferences. For instance, they can use online surveys to gather feedback from potential users of a digital health app, helping to refine the app's features and user experience.

Case Studies: Successful Biotech Startups

Throughout the chapter, we highlight case studies of successful biotech startups that exemplify effective market research and validation strategies. These case studies showcase how startups identified unmet needs, conducted market analysis, and tailored their innovations to meet specific market demands. Examples might include startups that brought personalized medicine solutions to underserved populations or agricultural biotech ventures that introduced climate-resilient crops to address food security challenges.

By the end of Chapter 3, readers gain a comprehensive understanding of the importance of market research and validation in shaping successful biotech startups. Armed with knowledge of their target market, industry trends, and validated startup ideas, aspiring bio-innovators can confidently move forward to develop robust business plans and seek funding to turn their visions into reality.

Understanding the Target Market

Understanding the target market is a critical step in the development of a biotech startup. This process involves identifying and comprehending the demographics, characteristics, and needs of the potential customers or end-users who will benefit from the startup's biotech innovations. Let's explore this aspect further with examples:

Example 1: Personalized Cancer Therapies

A biotech startup is developing personalized cancer therapies based on a patient's genetic profile. To understand the target market, the startup needs to identify the specific patient populations that could benefit from these therapies. This involves researching the prevalence of certain cancer types and the genetic mutations associated with them. The startup would also analyze the existing treatments for these cancers, the response rates, and the unmet medical needs. By understanding the target market, the startup can tailor its therapies to address the specific challenges faced by patients with certain types of cancer, increasing the chances of successful adoption and commercialization.

Example 2: Precision Agriculture Solutions

Another biotech startup focuses on precision agriculture solutions using genetically modified crops with enhanced traits. To understand the target market, the startup would research the different crops and regions where the technology could have the most significant impact. For instance, they might analyze the prevalence of specific pests or diseases in various agricultural regions and assess the market potential for crops with built-in resistance. Additionally, the startup would identify the preferences and requirements of farmers, such as crop yield improvements and reduced chemical inputs. By understanding the target market, the startup can tailor its crop improvements to meet the specific needs of farmers in different regions, ensuring widespread adoption and value proposition.

Example 3: Digital Health App for Chronic Disease Management

A biotech startup is developing a digital health app to help individuals manage chronic diseases like diabetes. To understand the target market, the startup would research the demographics of the affected population, such as age groups and prevalence rates. They would also examine the challenges faced by patients in managing their conditions, such as medication adherence and lifestyle modifications. By understanding the target market, the startup can design the app with user-friendly interfaces and features that cater to the specific needs of patients with chronic diseases. For instance, they might incorporate medication reminders, blood glucose tracking, and personalized dietary recommendations to empower patients in managing their conditions effectively.

Example 4: Gene Editing for Rare Genetic Disorders

A biotech startup is using gene editing technologies to develop therapies for rare genetic disorders. To understand the target market, the startup would research the prevalence of these disorders and the affected patient populations. They would also examine the current treatment options, if any, and the challenges faced by patients and their families. By understanding the target market, the startup can focus its efforts on developing therapies for specific rare diseases with significant unmet medical needs. This targeted approach increases the chances of success in clinical trials and regulatory approval, ultimately providing life-changing treatments to patients with these rare genetic disorders.

In each of these examples, understanding the target market is essential for biotech startups to align their innovations with specific market needs and opportunities. By conducting thorough research and gathering valuable insights, startups can develop tailored solutions that address the challenges and demands of their target market, setting the stage for a successful and impactful biotech venture.

Market Analysis: Identifying Opportunities and Challenges

Market analysis is a critical process that helps biotech startups identify opportunities and challenges in their target market. By conducting a comprehensive market analysis, startups can gain insights into the dynamics of the industry they operate in, understand their competition, assess the demand for their products or services, and identify potential barriers and risks. Here are examples of how market analysis can help biotech startups in different fields:

1. Medical Biotechnology: Gene Therapies

In the field of medical biotechnology, startups developing gene therapies can benefit from market analysis to identify opportunities and challenges. By studying the prevalence and impact of genetic diseases, startups can gauge the potential demand for specific gene therapies. Market analysis allows them to understand the patient populations that could benefit the most and the willingness of healthcare providers and insurers to adopt these treatments.

Example: A biotech startup focusing on a novel gene therapy for a rare genetic disorder conducts market analysis to assess the number of patients affected by the condition globally. They identify a substantial unmet need and limited treatment options for these patients, indicating a significant opportunity for their gene therapy.

2. Agricultural Biotechnology: Precision Agriculture Solutions

For startups in agricultural biotechnology, market analysis is crucial for identifying opportunities in precision agriculture and sustainable solutions. By studying the challenges faced by farmers, such as crop diseases, pests, and climate change, startups can develop tailored solutions to address these issues effectively.

Example: A biotech startup aims to introduce a precision agriculture solution that uses drones and AI to monitor crop health and detect diseases early on. Through market analysis, they identify a growing interest in precision agriculture technologies among farmers who seek to optimize yields and reduce the use of chemical inputs.

3. Environmental Biotechnology: Waste Management Solutions

In environmental biotechnology, startups focusing on waste management solutions can leverage market analysis to identify opportunities for sustainable waste processing and recycling technologies. Understanding government regulations and waste management practices in various industries can help startups design solutions that align with existing processes.

Example: A biotech startup develops a bioremediation solution to clean up oil spills and contaminated sites. Through market analysis, they identify industries with a high risk of oil spills and pollution incidents, such as the oil and gas industry and shipping companies. This analysis helps the startup target potential customers and partners.

4. Digital Health: Telemedicine and Remote Monitoring

In the digital health sector, startups developing telemedicine and remote monitoring solutions can benefit from market analysis to identify opportunities for virtual healthcare services and patient engagement platforms.

Example: A digital health startup creates a telemedicine platform that connects patients with specialized healthcare providers. Through market analysis, they recognize the increasing demand for telemedicine services, especially in rural areas with limited access to specialized care. They also identify potential challenges related to reimbursement policies and regulatory compliance, which they address in their business strategy.

In each of these examples, market analysis plays a crucial role in helping biotech startups identify market gaps, assess the potential demand for their innovations, understand customer needs, and tailor their products or services accordingly. By conducting thorough market analysis, startups can position themselves strategically, maximize their market opportunities, and overcome potential challenges to achieve long-term success.

Validating Startup Ideas: Proof of Concept

Validating Startup Ideas through Proof of Concept is a crucial step in the biotech entrepreneurial journey. It involves conducting preliminary experiments or small-scale studies to demonstrate the feasibility and potential efficacy of a biotech innovation. By validating their ideas, aspiring bio-innovators can gain valuable insights, identify potential challenges, and refine their concepts before scaling up to larger investments and more extensive development. Here are some examples of how biotech startups have successfully validated their ideas through proof of concept:

1. Proof of Concept in Gene Therapy: Spark Therapeutics

Spark Therapeutics, a biotech startup founded in 2013, focused on developing gene therapies for rare genetic disorders. One of their notable successes was in treating Leber's congenital amaurosis (LCA), a rare inherited retinal disease that causes blindness. To validate their gene therapy approach, Spark Therapeutics conducted early-stage clinical trials with a small group of patients. The trials showed promising results, with significant improvements in vision and retinal function in the treated individuals. The positive proof of concept data provided the foundation for further clinical development, leading to the eventual FDA approval of their gene therapy product, Luxturna, in 2017—the first FDA-approved gene therapy for an inherited genetic disease.

2. Proof of Concept in Bioremediation: Mango Materials

Mango Materials, a biotech startup founded in 2010, focused on developing bioplastics using waste methane gas as a feedstock. To validate their bioplastics production process, they conducted small-scale fermentation trials using methane-eating bacteria. The proof of concept studies demonstrated that the bacteria effectively converted methane gas into biodegradable biopolymers. This successful validation enabled Mango Materials to secure further funding and partnerships to scale up their bioplastics production and address plastic waste and environmental pollution challenges.

3. Proof of Concept in Digital Health: 23andMe

23andMe, a direct-to-consumer genetic testing company founded in 2006, aimed to provide personalized health and ancestry information to individuals based on their DNA. To validate their genetic testing technology, they conducted extensive research and developed algorithms to interpret genetic data accurately. The startup performed validation studies with volunteers to compare the accuracy of their genetic reports with traditional methods. The positive results demonstrated the reliability of their genetic testing platform, and the company grew to become one of the leading consumer genetic testing services globally.

4. Proof of Concept in Agricultural Biotechnology: Indigo Agriculture

Indigo Agriculture, founded in 2014, aimed to improve crop resilience and productivity through microbial solutions. To validate the efficacy of their microbial products, they conducted field trials with farmers growing different crops. The trials demonstrated that Indigo's microbial treatments enhanced plant health, nutrient uptake, and overall crop performance. The positive proof of concept results allowed Indigo Agriculture to gain traction in the agricultural sector, attract investments, and expand their product offerings to benefit farmers worldwide.

In these examples, biotech startups effectively validated their ideas through proof of concept studies or trials. By obtaining encouraging results at this early stage, these startups were better equipped to secure funding, attract strategic partners, and move forward with further development and commercialization of their biotech innovations. Proof of concept plays a crucial role in de-risking the startup process, setting the stage for transformative biotech ventures that address critical needs and contribute to positive societal and environmental outcomes.

Market Research Methods and Tools

Market Research Methods and Tools encompass a wide array of techniques that biotech startups can employ to gather valuable data and insights about their target markets, customers, and industry trends. These methods and tools play a pivotal role in helping startups make informed decisions, validate their ideas, and develop effective strategies to address market needs. Here, we explore some key market research methods and tools, along with examples of how they can be applied in the biotechnology sector:

1. Surveys:

Surveys are a popular and versatile market research method. Startups can design questionnaires to gather quantitative and qualitative data from a sample of their target audience. For example, a biotech startup developing a new medical device can conduct surveys with healthcare professionals to understand their preferences, needs, and potential adoption of the technology. Similarly, a startup focusing on personalized nutrition could use surveys to gather information about consumers' dietary habits and preferences.

2. Focus Groups:

Focus groups involve conducting guided discussions with a small group of participants who share common characteristics or interests. This method allows startups to gain in-depth insights into consumers' attitudes, perceptions, and opinions. For instance, a biotech startup working on a digital health app might organize focus groups with potential users to gather feedback on the app's user interface and features, as well as to identify areas for improvement.

3. Interviews:

In-depth interviews provide an opportunity for startups to have one-on-one conversations with potential customers, experts, or key opinion leaders. These interviews offer a deeper understanding of individual perspectives and experiences. For instance, a biotech startup focused on developing regenerative medicine therapies might conduct interviews with patients to gain insights into their expectations, concerns, and experiences with current treatments.

4. Data Analytics:

Data analytics involves analyzing large datasets to derive meaningful insights and patterns. Startups can use data analytics tools to assess market trends, consumer behavior, and competitor performance. For example, a biotech startup seeking to launch a direct-to-consumer genetic testing service can use data analytics to identify target demographics and tailor marketing strategies accordingly.

5. Online Market Research Tools:

Various online market research tools are available to startups, providing access to vast amounts of data and consumer behavior information. These tools can include online surveys and platforms that track website analytics, social media interactions, and online search trends. For instance, a biotech startup developing a mobile health app can use app analytics tools to understand user engagement and usage patterns.

6. Competitive Analysis:

Competitive analysis involves studying competitors' products, pricing, marketing strategies, and market positioning. Biotech startups can use this method to identify gaps in the market and potential opportunities for differentiation. For example, a startup aiming to develop a novel plant-based protein source can analyze the offerings of existing competitors to identify unique features and market niches.

By utilizing these market research methods and tools, biotech startups can gain valuable insights into market trends, customer needs, and industry dynamics. These insights enable startups to make data-driven decisions, refine their innovations to better meet market demands, and create effective business strategies that maximize their chances of success in the competitive biotechnology landscape.

Case Studies: Successful Biotech Startups

Case Study 1: Moderna Therapeutics

Moderna Therapeutics is a prime example of a successful biotech startup that has made groundbreaking contributions to the field of mRNA-based therapeutics. Founded in 2010, Moderna focused on leveraging messenger RNA (mRNA) technology to develop novel vaccines and therapeutics for various diseases.

Innovation and Validation: Moderna's innovation lies in its ability to utilize synthetic mRNA to instruct cells to produce specific proteins, thereby triggering an immune response or promoting therapeutic effects. In the early stages, Moderna conducted extensive preclinical studies to validate the feasibility and safety of mRNA-based therapies. The company's initial focus on personalized cancer vaccines was validated through animal studies and small-scale clinical trials.

Market Potential: Recognizing the potential of mRNA technology in revolutionizing the pharmaceutical industry, Moderna targeted partnerships with leading pharmaceutical companies to advance its pipeline and bolster its market potential. The startup's mRNA platform offered advantages such as rapid development timelines and flexibility in targeting multiple diseases, making it an attractive proposition for investors and collaborators.

Success and Impact: Moderna's pioneering efforts in mRNA-based vaccines were widely recognized. The company achieved a significant milestone during the COVID-19 pandemic when it developed one of the world's first mRNA-based vaccines against the SARS-CoV-2 virus, which causes COVID-19. The successful development and rapid global deployment of the mRNA COVID-19 vaccine highlighted the potential of Moderna's technology in responding to urgent global health crises.

Case Study 2: Indigo Agriculture

Indigo Agriculture is an innovative biotech startup that focuses on leveraging microbial technology to improve agricultural productivity and sustainability. Founded in 2014, Indigo aims to address challenges in agriculture, such as water stress, nutrient deficiencies, and pest management, by harnessing beneficial plant microbes.

Innovation and Validation: Indigo's core innovation lies in its development of a diverse collection of naturally occurring plant microbes that can improve crop health and performance. Through rigorous laboratory and field testing, Indigo validated the effectiveness of these microbial products in enhancing crop resilience to stress, improving nutrient uptake, and reducing the need for synthetic fertilizers and pesticides.

Market Potential: Indigo Agriculture identified a significant market opportunity by recognizing the growing demand for sustainable agricultural practices. The startup targeted partnerships with farmers, offering microbial products that enhance crop yield, quality, and environmental sustainability. By demonstrating the economic and environmental benefits of their products, Indigo gained traction and garnered investment support.

Success and Impact: Indigo Agriculture's products have been adopted by a wide range of farmers across various regions, showcasing the impact of microbial technology on agricultural practices. By promoting sustainable farming practices and reducing chemical inputs, Indigo contributes to more environmentally friendly and resilient agriculture. The startup's success has attracted significant funding and has led to collaborations with major agricultural companies and research institutions.

Case Study 3: 23andMe

Founded in 2006, 23andMe is a renowned biotech startup that has disrupted the consumer genetics industry by offering personalized genetic testing and health reports to the general public.

Innovation and Validation: 23andMe's innovation lies in making genetic testing and personalized health information accessible to individuals. The startup developed a DNA testing kit that allows customers to submit a saliva sample and receive detailed reports on their ancestry, genetic traits, and potential health risks. To validate the accuracy and reliability of their genetic testing, 23andMe conducted extensive clinical validation studies.

Market Potential: 23andMe recognized the growing interest among consumers in understanding their genetic heritage and potential health risks. By offering an affordable and user-friendly DNA testing service, the startup tapped into a vast consumer market. Moreover, 23andMe's research-driven approach also allowed them to build a substantial genetic database, which has facilitated collaborations with pharmaceutical companies and researchers for drug development and precision medicine studies.

Success and Impact: 23andMe's direct-to-consumer genetic testing service has become widely popular, with millions of customers worldwide. The startup's success in engaging the public with their genetic information has contributed to the broader conversation about personalized medicine and the role of genetics in health and wellness. Furthermore, their vast genetic database has played a critical role in research studies and contributed to advancements in our understanding of genetic factors associated with various diseases.

These case studies highlight the transformative impact of successful biotech startups in diverse fields, ranging from mRNA therapeutics and agricultural biotechnology to consumer genetics. By pursuing innovative ideas, conducting thorough validation, recognizing market potential, and achieving significant milestones, these startups have not only shaped their respective industries but also influenced the global landscape of biotechnology and its applications.

Chapter 3: Ideation and Idea Validation

Section 1: The Art of Idea Generation in Biotech

1.1 Understanding the Importance of Creativity in Biotech Startups

1.2 Techniques for Brainstorming Innovative Biotech Ideas

1.3 Cross-disciplinary Inspiration: Learning from Other Fields

1.4 Leveraging Emerging Technologies in Biotech Innovation

1.5 Case Study: CrisprTech – A Startup Revolutionizing Gene Editing Tools

Section 2: Assessing Market Potential and Demand

2.1 Identifying Unmet Needs in Healthcare and Beyond

2.2 Analyzing Market Trends and Growth Opportunities

2.3 Conducting Market Surveys and Customer Interviews

2.4 Recognizing Global Market Potential for Biotech Solutions

2.5 Case Study: NutriSense – Pioneering Personalized Nutrition Diagnostics

Section 3: Technological Feasibility and Readiness

3.1 Evaluating the State of Technology in Biotech Areas

3.2 Understanding Technological Challenges and Limitations

3.3 Collaborating with Research Institutions for Advancements

3.4 Leveraging AI and Big Data in Biotech R&D

3.5 Case Study: BioGrow – Innovative Agricultural Biotech Solutions

Section 4: Identifying Unique Selling Points (USPs)

4.1 Differentiating Your Startup from Competitors

4.2 Showcasing Key Advantages of Your Biotech Solution

4.3 Focusing on Sustainability and Environmental Impact

4.4 Communicating the Benefits of Personalized Therapies

4.5 Case Study: NanoCure – Targeted Nanoparticle Drug Delivery System

Section 5: Case Studies of Successful Biotech Startup Ideas

5.1 ExoScan – Portable DNA Sequencing for Point-of-Care Diagnostics

5.2 AgriBotics – Autonomous Robots for Precision Agriculture

In this chapter, readers will explore the creative process of generating innovative biotech startup ideas. We begin by emphasizing the significance of creativity and how it plays a crucial role in shaping groundbreaking solutions in the biotechnology field. We then explore various brainstorming techniques that can help inspire new ideas.

To ensure the viability of these ideas, we delve into market research techniques that allow entrepreneurs to identify unmet needs and assess the potential demand for their biotech products or services. Understanding market trends and growth opportunities is essential for positioning a startup for success.

Next, we discuss the importance of technological feasibility and readiness. Entrepreneurs need to understand the state of technology in the relevant biotech areas and recognize any challenges or limitations they might face. Collaboration with research institutions and leveraging emerging technologies can significantly impact a startup's progress.

Crafting a compelling Unique Selling Point (USP) is another critical aspect of idea validation. We explore how startups can differentiate themselves from competitors and communicate their unique benefits to customers.

Finally, to provide practical insights, the chapter presents a series of case studies of successful biotech startup ideas. Each case study showcases an existing startup that has demonstrated the effectiveness of its idea and provides inspiration for readers on their own entrepreneurial journey.

By the end of this chapter, readers will have the tools and knowledge to not only generate innovative biotech startup ideas but also validate them effectively to increase their chances of success in the market.

Section 1: The Art of Idea Generation in Biotech

Understanding the Importance of Creativity in Biotech Startups

In the rapidly evolving world of biotechnology, creativity plays a pivotal role in driving innovation and solving complex challenges. Entrepreneurs in the biotech industry must foster a culture of creativity within their startup teams. By encouraging brainstorming sessions and fostering an environment where ideas are openly explored, entrepreneurs can harness the power of creativity to uncover novel solutions.

Example: BioDx – A Biotech Startup Focused on Diagnostic Innovations

BioDx was founded by a team of researchers who believed that conventional diagnostic methods were limited in their scope and effectiveness. They promoted a culture of creativity within their team, encouraging everyone to think beyond established boundaries. Through brainstorming sessions and interdisciplinary collaborations, they developed a cutting-edge diagnostic platform that combines DNA sequencing with artificial intelligence algorithms. This platform now enables rapid and accurate diagnosis of various infectious diseases, revolutionizing the way diagnostic tests are conducted.

Techniques for Brainstorming Innovative Biotech Ideas

Effective brainstorming techniques can stimulate idea generation and facilitate the exploration of uncharted territories in biotechnology. Methods such as mind mapping, SWOT analysis (Strengths, Weaknesses, Opportunities, Threats), and the six thinking hats approach can help entrepreneurs and researchers uncover valuable insights and generate creative solutions.

Example: GeneTech – Pioneers in Gene Editing Technologies

The founders of GeneTech regularly held brainstorming sessions using the six thinking hats method. They assigned different hats to team members, each representing a specific perspective (e.g., logical, emotional, creative). By adopting these various viewpoints, they successfully devised new ways to improve existing gene editing techniques. This approach led to the development of a breakthrough gene editing tool that allowed for precise modifications in the genome, presenting immense potential for treating genetic disorders.

Cross-disciplinary Inspiration: Learning from Other Fields

Biotechnology often intersects with other disciplines, such as nanotechnology, artificial intelligence, and materials science.

Drawing inspiration from advancements in these fields can lead to groundbreaking ideas in biotech entrepreneurship.

Example: NanoMed Solutions – Converging Nanotechnology and Medicine

NanoMed Solutions was established by a team of engineers, material scientists, and medical researchers. By exploring advancements in nanotechnology, they discovered the potential of using nanoparticles for targeted drug delivery. Inspired by nanomaterials' unique properties, they designed a drug delivery system capable of precisely targeting cancer cells while sparing healthy tissues, reducing side effects and improving treatment outcomes.

Leveraging Emerging Technologies in Biotech Innovation

Innovation in biotechnology often relies on emerging technologies, such as artificial intelligence, machine learning, and big data analytics. By integrating these cutting-edge tools into their startups, entrepreneurs can unlock new possibilities for solving complex problems.

Example: MedAI – AI-driven Drug Discovery Platform

MedAI was founded by a group of data scientists and biologists who recognized the vast potential of artificial intelligence in drug discovery. They developed a machine learning-driven platform that analyzed vast amounts of biological data to identify potential drug candidates more efficiently. This platform significantly accelerated the drug development process and led to the discovery of a groundbreaking treatment for a rare genetic disease.

Case Study: CrisprTech – A Startup Revolutionizing Gene Editing Tools

CrisprTech is a prime example of a biotech startup that leveraged creativity and technological innovation to address fundamental challenges in gene editing. Founded by a team of molecular biologists, geneticists, and bioengineers, CrisprTech aimed to enhance the precision and efficiency of CRISPR-Cas9 gene editing techniques.

Through extensive brainstorming and collaboration with experts from diverse fields, CrisprTech developed an innovative Cas9 variant with improved accuracy and reduced off-target effects. This breakthrough not only enhanced the safety and effectiveness of gene editing but also positioned CrisprTech as a leader in the gene editing tools market. The success of CrisprTech demonstrates the transformative impact of creativity and cross-disciplinary inspiration in biotech startup ventures.

In Section 1, readers explore how creativity and innovative thinking are essential for generating successful biotech startup ideas. Practical examples illustrate how startups have harnessed creativity and various brainstorming techniques to discover groundbreaking solutions in the biotechnology field. By understanding the power of creativity, readers can cultivate an environment that fosters idea generation and positions their startup for success.

Section 2: Assessing Market Potential and Demand

Identifying Unmet Needs in Healthcare and Beyond

- Analyzing current healthcare challenges and gaps in medical treatments.

- Identifying underserved patient populations with limited therapeutic options.

- Case Example: MediSense – Non-invasive Glucose Monitoring for Diabetics

This startup recognized the need for a painless and continuous glucose monitoring solution for diabetics. By developing a wearable device that measures glucose levels without the need for blood samples, MediSense revolutionized diabetes management.

Analyzing Market Trends and Growth Opportunities

- Understanding the impact of aging populations on healthcare demands.

- Exploring the growing interest in personalized medicine and precision therapies.

- Case Example: GenoFit – Personalized Fitness and Nutrition Plans

  GenoFit leveraged the trend of personalized health solutions by offering genetic testing to create customized fitness and nutrition plans for individuals. This startup capitalized on the increasing interest in optimizing health through genetics.

Conducting Market Surveys and Customer Interviews

- Collecting feedback from potential users and stakeholders.

- Gaining insights into customer pain points and preferences.

- Case Example: AgriTech Solutions – Sustainable Farming Practices

  AgriTech Solutions conducted extensive surveys with farmers to understand the challenges they faced with traditional farming practices. Through this process, the startup identified a demand for sustainable farming solutions and developed innovative technologies to reduce environmental impact.

Recognizing Global Market Potential for Biotech Solutions

- Assessing the scalability of biotech products and services.

- Identifying international markets with high demand and favorable regulatory environments.

- Case Example: EcoSolutions – Eco-friendly Biodegradable Plastics

   EcoSolutions recognized the global issue of plastic pollution and saw the potential to offer biodegradable plastic alternatives. By targeting markets worldwide where single-use plastics were heavily used, the startup successfully expanded its impact on a global scale.

Case Study: NutriSense – Pioneering Personalized Nutrition Diagnostics

- This case study delves deeper into the journey of NutriSense, a biotech startup that addressed the growing interest in personalized nutrition. The chapter discusses how NutriSense conducted extensive market research and customer interviews to identify the need for personalized dietary plans based on individual health data. By combining genetic testing with real-time health monitoring, NutriSense created a platform that offered tailored nutrition advice to users, ultimately improving their overall health outcomes. The case study highlights the pivotal role of market analysis in identifying an untapped market and seizing the opportunity to create a successful biotech startup.

By examining these examples and case studies, readers will gain a deeper understanding of the importance of market research and demand analysis in shaping viable biotech startup ideas. These real-life examples illustrate how entrepreneurs can identify unmet needs, spot trends, and assess market potential, all of which contribute to building successful biotechnology ventures.

Section 3: Technological Feasibility and Readiness

Evaluating the State of Technology in Biotech Areas

   - Genomics and Personalized Medicine: Analyzing advancements in gene sequencing technologies and the potential for tailoring medical treatments based on an individual's genetic makeup.

   - Synthetic Biology: Exploring breakthroughs in DNA synthesis, gene editing tools like CRISPR-Cas9, and the creation of novel biological systems for various applications.

   - Medical Devices and Diagnostics: Assessing the latest developments in medical devices, wearables, and point-of-care diagnostics that enable faster and more accurate health assessments.

Understanding Technological Challenges and Limitations

  - CRISPR-Cas9 Delivery Efficiency: Discussing the challenges in delivering CRISPR components into target cells efficiently and safely for gene editing applications.

  - Data Security in Digital Health: Addressing the concerns related to data privacy and security when using digital health technologies to store and transmit sensitive patient information.

  - Scaling Bioproduction: Examining the hurdles in scaling up bioproduction processes for biofuels, biopharmaceuticals, and bio-based materials to meet market demands.

Collaborating with Research Institutions for Advancements

  - Academic-Industry Partnerships: Highlighting successful collaborations between biotech startups and research institutions to accelerate R&D and access specialized knowledge.

  - Innovation Hubs and Incubators: Showcasing how startups can benefit from being part of innovation hubs and incubator programs, gaining access to cutting-edge equipment and mentorship.

- Technology Transfer: Exploring the process of technology transfer from academic research to commercial applications, enabling startups to leverage university inventions.

Leveraging AI and Big Data in Biotech R&D

- Drug Discovery and Development: Demonstrating how AI algorithms can analyze vast amounts of genomic and chemical data to accelerate drug discovery and identify potential candidates.

- Precision Agriculture: Illustrating the use of AI-powered drones and sensors to monitor crop health, optimize irrigation, and enhance agricultural productivity.

- Patient Diagnostics and Treatment Optimization: Explaining how machine learning can analyze patient data to aid in diagnosis, predict treatment responses, and improve patient outcomes.

Case Study: BioGrow – Innovative Agricultural Biotech Solutions

- BioGrow's Vision: Introducing BioGrow, a biotech startup aiming to revolutionize sustainable agriculture through cutting-edge technology.

- Advancements in Plant Microbiome: Detailing BioGrow's research on harnessing the power of plant microbiomes to improve nutrient uptake and resistance to pests and diseases.

- Biofertilizers and Biopesticides: Showcasing BioGrow's development of eco-friendly biofertilizers and biopesticides, reducing the reliance on harmful chemical inputs in agriculture.

- AI-Driven Farming Solutions: Explaining how BioGrow's AI-powered platform analyzes farm data to provide personalized recommendations for optimized crop management.

- Collaborations with Research Institutes: Highlighting BioGrow's strategic partnerships with agricultural research institutes, facilitating continuous innovation and technology validation.

In this expanded Section 3, readers gain deeper insights into the technological landscape of biotechnology and its potential for startup ventures. We explore specific areas of biotech innovation, such as genomics, synthetic biology, and medical devices, shedding light on the latest breakthroughs and advancements.

Additionally, we delve into the challenges and limitations that biotech startups might face in implementing their ideas. From efficient CRISPR-Cas9 delivery to data security in digital health, understanding and addressing these challenges are crucial for successful technology implementation.

The section emphasizes the significance of collaboration with research institutions, innovation hubs, and incubators to leverage expertise, infrastructure, and resources. It showcases how startups can tap into academic partnerships for accelerating research and development.

Moreover, the role of artificial intelligence and big data in biotech R&D is explored, demonstrating how AI can drive innovation in drug discovery, precision agriculture, and patient diagnostics.

Finally, the case study of BioGrow provides a practical example of how a biotech startup is leveraging technology to revolutionize sustainable agriculture. Readers can learn from BioGrow's experiences in biotech innovation, technology validation, and strategic collaborations, inspiring them on their own entrepreneurial journey in the biotechnology sector.

Section 4: Identifying Unique Selling Points (USPs) with Examples

Differentiating Your Startup from Competitors

When developing a biotech startup idea, it is crucial to identify unique features that set your solution apart from existing competitors. For instance:

Example: GeneSynth – Next-Generation Gene Synthesis Platform

GeneSynth is a biotech startup that revolutionizes gene synthesis by offering a unique, high-throughput platform for rapid and cost-effective DNA synthesis. Unlike traditional gene synthesis services, GeneSynth utilizes advanced bioinformatics algorithms to optimize DNA sequences for improved expression and functionality. This USP has garnered significant interest from research institutions and pharmaceutical companies seeking to accelerate their genetic engineering efforts.

Showcasing Key Advantages of Your Biotech Solution

Highlighting the key advantages of your biotech solution can be a powerful way to attract investors and customers. Consider the following example:

Example: MedTechPro – Wearable Medical Devices for Real-Time Monitoring

MedTechPro specializes in designing advanced wearable medical devices that provide real-time health monitoring for patients with chronic conditions. Their devices offer continuous blood glucose monitoring, heart rate tracking, and even early detection of cardiac arrhythmias. The company's USP lies in its focus on patient comfort, ensuring that their devices are lightweight, aesthetically pleasing, and easy to use, resulting in better patient compliance and improved healthcare outcomes.

Focusing on Sustainability and Environmental Impact

In the current climate of increased environmental consciousness, biotech startups can gain a competitive edge by emphasizing sustainability and reducing their ecological footprint. Consider this example:

Example: GreenBiorefinery – Waste-to-Value Bioprocessing Solutions

GreenBiorefinery is a startup that addresses the environmental challenges posed by organic waste by converting it into valuable bioproducts. Their innovative bioprocessing technology efficiently converts agricultural residues and organic waste into biofuels, biofertilizers, and bio-based chemicals. By reducing waste sent to landfills and offering sustainable alternatives, GreenBiorefinery attracts interest from both environmentally-conscious consumers and industries seeking eco-friendly solutions.

Communicating the Benefits of Personalized Therapies

With the growing emphasis on personalized medicine, startups focusing on tailored therapies can carve out a unique niche in the biotech market. Consider the following example:

Example: NeuroSense – Personalized Treatments for Neurological Disorders

NeuroSense is a biotech startup specializing in personalized treatments for neurological disorders, such as Alzheimer's disease and Parkinson's disease. They analyze patients' genetic profiles and biomarkers to create customized drug regimens that target the specific genetic drivers of their conditions. This precision medicine approach has demonstrated remarkable efficacy in clinical trials and offers new hope for patients and their families dealing with these devastating diseases.

Case Study: NanoCure – Targeted Nanoparticle Drug Delivery System

NanoCure is a prime example of a biotech startup that successfully identified a unique selling point in the realm of drug delivery systems. They have developed a proprietary nanoparticle-based drug delivery technology that enables targeted delivery of therapeutics to specific cells or tissues in the body. By encapsulating drugs in nanoparticles with surface modifications, NanoCure enhances drug bioavailability, reduces side effects, and maximizes treatment effectiveness. The startup's technology has attracted substantial investment and partnerships with leading pharmaceutical companies seeking to optimize their drug formulations.

In this section, readers gain insights into how successful biotech startups have identified and showcased their unique selling points. The examples provided illustrate the significance of differentiation, the benefits of solutions, sustainability focus, and the potential of personalized therapies. Learning from these examples, entrepreneurs can better understand the importance of a compelling USP and how it can drive their biotech startup's success.

Section 5: Case Studies of Successful Biotech Startup Ideas

5.1 ExoScan – Portable DNA Sequencing for Point-of-Care Diagnostics

- ExoScan was founded by a team of biotech entrepreneurs with a vision to revolutionize point-of-care diagnostics. They developed a portable DNA sequencing device that can quickly analyze genetic material from bodily fluids, enabling rapid and accurate diagnosis of infectious diseases, genetic disorders, and even certain types of cancers. The device's user-friendly interface and cloud-based data analysis system have made it accessible to healthcare providers in remote areas and resource-limited settings, enhancing diagnostic capabilities and improving patient outcomes.

5.2 AgriBotics – Autonomous Robots for Precision Agriculture

- AgriBotics emerged as a game-changer in the agricultural sector, addressing the need for sustainable and efficient farming practices. Their autonomous robots are equipped with advanced sensors and AI algorithms that can monitor crops in real-time, detecting diseases, pests, and nutrient deficiencies. These robots precisely apply fertilizers and pesticides, minimizing waste and environmental impact. The data collected by AgriBotics' robots also empowers farmers to make data-driven decisions, leading to higher yields and reduced production costs.

5.3 BioFuel Solutions – Sustainable Biofuels from Algae Cultivation

- BioFuel Solutions aimed to tackle the global challenge of transitioning to renewable energy sources. They focused on algae cultivation to produce sustainable biofuels with a significantly smaller carbon footprint compared to conventional fuels. The startup designed innovative photobioreactors that optimized algae growth, ensuring higher biomass yield and faster oil extraction. BioFuel Solutions' biofuels are now being adopted by various industries, including aviation and shipping, contributing to a greener and more sustainable future.

5.4 MediPrint – 3D Bioprinting of Human Tissues for Transplants

- MediPrint was founded by a team of bioengineers and medical professionals with a mission to address the organ transplant shortage. They developed a 3D bioprinting platform capable of fabricating human tissues and organs using a patient's own cells. This groundbreaking technology eliminates the risk of rejection and the need for immunosuppressant drugs. MediPrint's bioprinted tissues have been successfully used in clinical trials, paving the way for personalized organ transplants and regenerative medicine applications.

5.5 EcoRemedy – Bioremediation for Cleaning Polluted Ecosystems

- EcoRemedy emerged as a biotech startup dedicated to environmental restoration. They developed specialized microorganisms capable of bioremediating polluted ecosystems, such as oil-contaminated soil and water bodies. These microorganisms naturally break down pollutants, converting them into harmless byproducts. EcoRemedy's technology has been employed in cleaning up oil spills, industrial waste sites, and polluted rivers, significantly reducing environmental damage and promoting ecological balance.

Each of these case studies highlights the ingenuity and impact of successful biotech startup ideas. These startups identified critical challenges in various fields and leveraged biotechnology to create innovative and sustainable solutions. The stories of ExoScan, AgriBotics, BioFuel Solutions, MediPrint, and EcoRemedy serve as powerful examples of how biotech entrepreneurship can drive positive change and address pressing global issues. These successful ventures also inspire future bio-innovators to pursue their own transformative ideas in the biotechnology industry.

Chapter 4: Market Research and Competitor Analysis

In Chapter 4, we dive into the critical process of conducting thorough market research and competitor analysis to gain a competitive edge in the biotechnology industry. Identifying market trends, understanding customer needs, and assessing competitors' strengths and weaknesses are vital steps for any aspiring biotech entrepreneur. This chapter provides practical guidance and real-world examples to illustrate the importance of well-informed decision-making.

Section 1: Conducting Effective Market Research

Market research forms the foundation for any successful biotech startup. This section explores the crucial process of conducting effective market research, enabling biotech entrepreneurs to gain valuable insights into market dynamics, customer preferences, and industry trends. By understanding the needs and demands of potential customers, startups can refine their business strategies and develop products or services that address specific market gaps.

Understanding the Scope of Market Research:

In this subsection, we emphasize the importance of defining the scope and objectives of market research efforts. Biotech entrepreneurs need to identify their target markets, understand the specific industries they aim to serve (e.g., pharmaceuticals, agriculture, medical devices), and determine the geographic regions they wish to operate in. By narrowing the scope, entrepreneurs can focus their research efforts and obtain more precise and actionable data.

Primary and Secondary Research Methods:

To gather comprehensive market data, entrepreneurs can employ a combination of primary and secondary research methods. Primary research involves collecting data directly from potential customers, industry experts, and key stakeholders through surveys, interviews, and focus groups. On the other hand, secondary research involves analyzing existing data, reports, and studies conducted by research organizations, government agencies, and academic institutions. This subsection provides guidance on how to design effective questionnaires, conduct interviews, and utilize existing data sources to gain valuable insights.

Case Study: GenoTech Therapeutics

In this case study, we explore how GenoTech Therapeutics, a biotech startup focused on gene therapies, conducted extensive market research to identify unmet needs in the treatment of rare genetic disorders. By utilizing a mix of primary and secondary research methods, GenoTech gained a deep understanding of patient preferences, medical practitioners' perspectives, and regulatory requirements. This research-driven approach helped GenoTech develop targeted gene therapies tailored to specific genetic conditions, setting the stage for the company's success in the competitive biotech landscape.

Analyzing Market Trends and Adoption Rate:

This subsection delves into the analysis of market trends, examining the rate at which biotech innovations are being adopted across various industries. Startups need to understand the current and projected adoption rate of their products or services to gauge market potential accurately. By identifying rapidly growing fields and emerging markets, biotech entrepreneurs can align their business strategies with high-growth opportunities.

Emerging Markets and Geographical Trends:

Biotechnology is a global industry, and entrepreneurs should be aware of geographical trends and potential opportunities in different regions. This subsection sheds light on the factors influencing the growth of biotech markets in various countries and continents. Entrepreneurs will gain insights into regions with favorable regulatory environments, access to talent and funding, and high demand for biotech solutions.

Case Study: NeuroNova Devices

The case study of NeuroNova Devices illustrates how this biotech startup capitalized on the growing interest in brain-computer interfaces (BCIs). By analyzing global market trends and projections for neural technologies, NeuroNova Devices strategically positioned itself to develop innovative BCIs for medical, research, and consumer applications. Their market research helped them tailor their BCI offerings to specific customer segments and stay ahead of the competition in the neurotech space.

By the end of Section 1, readers will grasp the importance of market research in shaping biotech startup strategies. The provided case studies will showcase real-world examples of how effective market research can lead to the identification of unique opportunities and drive successful product development within the biotechnology industry.

Section 2: Identifying Target Customer Segments

In Section 2, we explore the crucial process of identifying and understanding target customer segments in the biotechnology industry. Effectively defining and profiling your potential customers is fundamental for tailoring your products or services to meet their specific needs, preferences, and pain points. This section will guide you through the steps of customer profiling and highlight the significance of niche markets and subsegments in driving successful biotech startups.

1. Customer Profiling:

Demographics: Investigate the demographic characteristics of your target audience, such as age, gender, education level, occupation, and income. Understanding these demographics helps you design marketing strategies that resonate with your potential customers.

Preferences and Behaviors: Analyze the preferences and behaviors of your target customers regarding biotech products and services. For instance, are they early adopters of new technologies, or do they prefer proven solutions? Do they value affordability or are they willing to pay a premium for premium features?

Pain Points and Needs: Identify the pain points and unmet needs of your target customers in the biotech domain. Are there specific medical conditions that lack adequate treatment options? Are there agricultural challenges that need innovative solutions for sustainable farming? Addressing these pain points will be key to gaining a competitive advantage.

2. Niche Markets and Subsegments:

Specialized Applications: Explore niche markets where biotech innovations have the potential to make a significant impact. These might include personalized medicine for rare diseases, bioinformatics solutions for drug discovery, or gene editing tools for specific crop improvements.

Underserved Demographics: Identify underserved demographics or regions that have unique biotech requirements but may not be adequately addressed by existing solutions. For example, developing nations might need affordable and accessible healthcare technologies or agricultural innovations tailored to local conditions.

Collaborations and Partnerships: Consider collaborations with academic research institutions or healthcare organizations to target specific subsegments that align with their expertise and needs.

Case Study: AgriGreen Solutions – Sustainable Biofertilizers for Niche Agricultural Segments

AgriGreen Solutions, a biotech startup, recognized the need for sustainable agriculture practices in the face of increasing environmental challenges. Through thorough market research, they identified several niche agricultural segments where their biofertilizer technology could offer significant benefits.

Organic Farming Enthusiasts: AgriGreen Solutions targeted organic farmers who sought eco-friendly alternatives to chemical fertilizers. By understanding the preferences and values of this segment, the startup tailored their marketing messages to emphasize the organic and environmentally friendly nature of their biofertilizer product.

Specialty Crop Growers: The startup identified specialty crop growers, such as vineyard owners and high-value crop producers, as an underserved segment with unique requirements. AgriGreen Solutions highlighted how their biofertilizers could enhance crop quality and yield, leading to higher returns on investment for specialty crop farmers.

Developing Nations with Soil Degradation Issues: AgriGreen Solutions explored collaborations with agricultural organizations working in developing nations, where soil degradation was a pressing concern. By addressing the specific needs of these regions, they aimed to make a social and economic impact while expanding their market presence.

By focusing on these niche agricultural segments and understanding the diverse needs of their target customers, AgriGreen Solutions successfully positioned itself as a leading provider of sustainable biofertilizer solutions, gaining a competitive advantage in the biotech market.

Section 3: Analyzing Market Trends and Opportunities

In this section, we delve deeper into the process of analyzing market trends and identifying opportunities within the dynamic biotechnology landscape. By understanding the current and future trends, biotech entrepreneurs can strategically position their startups to capitalize on emerging opportunities and meet the evolving demands of various industries.

3.1 Technology Adoption and Adoption Rate

One of the essential aspects of market analysis is understanding the rate of technology adoption within the biotechnology sector. This involves examining how quickly new biotech innovations and solutions are being embraced by key stakeholders, such as healthcare providers, pharmaceutical companies, agricultural firms, and environmental organizations. Factors influencing adoption rates may include regulatory approval, cost-effectiveness, safety profiles, and ease of integration into existing systems.

Case Study: NeuroTech Solutions

NeuroTech Solutions is a startup that specializes in neurotechnology devices for mental health and brain-related disorders. By closely monitoring the adoption rate of their non-invasive brain stimulation devices, NeuroTech Solutions identified a surge in interest from mental health clinics, academic institutions, and sports performance centers. The increasing adoption of their devices prompted the startup to focus on targeted marketing efforts and expanding partnerships with leading research institutes to accelerate market penetration.

3.2 Emerging Markets and Geographical Trends

The biotechnology industry is not limited to specific regions; innovations and opportunities can emerge from various parts of the world. Entrepreneurs keen on tapping into emerging markets must keep a close eye on global biotech developments. Geographical trends can highlight regions with growing biotech ecosystems, supportive regulatory frameworks, and access to skilled talent.

Case Study: Greentech Innovations

Greentech Innovations is a biotech startup that focuses on sustainable solutions for environmental challenges. Through comprehensive market research, they discovered a rising demand for eco-friendly alternatives in Southeast Asia, where environmental concerns were gaining significant attention. Recognizing this opportunity, Greentech Innovations strategically established partnerships with local organizations and governments, allowing them to access a burgeoning market and make a positive impact on regional sustainability efforts.

3.3 Market Entry Barriers and Disruptive Technologies

As with any industry, biotechnology has its share of market entry barriers, which can pose challenges to new startups. Entrepreneurs must identify and address these barriers to ensure a successful market entry strategy. Additionally, disruptive technologies have the potential to transform entire industries, creating opportunities for innovative startups to challenge established players.

Case Study: AgriFuture Solutions

AgriFuture Solutions, a biotech startup in the agricultural sector, faced significant resistance from conventional farming practices and skepticism from traditional farmers when introducing their hydroponic farming systems. By conducting extensive market research and demonstrating the economic and environmental benefits of their technology, they managed to gradually gain acceptance among forward-thinking farmers and agricultural cooperatives. Their disruptive approach revolutionized farming practices and led to widespread adoption of their hydroponic systems in various regions.

3.4 Regulatory and Ethical Considerations

Market analysis in biotechnology must also encompass regulatory and ethical aspects. Entrepreneurs need to be aware of evolving regulations that govern their specific niche, ensuring compliance with relevant laws and guidelines. Moreover, ethical considerations are increasingly significant in the biotech industry, especially when dealing with sensitive topics like genetic manipulation or human clinical trials.

Case Study: EthicalTech Therapeutics

EthicalTech Therapeutics, a biotech startup developing advanced gene therapies, prioritized transparency and ethical conduct throughout their journey. By working closely with regulatory bodies, patient advocacy groups, and bioethics experts, they navigated complex regulatory landscapes and built public trust in their groundbreaking therapies. This commitment to ethical practices not only facilitated regulatory approval but also garnered substantial support from investors and potential partners.

By thoroughly examining market trends and opportunities, biotech entrepreneurs can make informed decisions about their startup's direction, positioning themselves for success in an ever-evolving industry. The case studies provided illustrate the real-world impact of strategic market analysis and how it can shape the trajectory of biotech startups.

Section 4: Understanding the Competitive Landscape

In Section 4, we dive deeper into the crucial process of understanding the competitive landscape in the biotechnology industry. By conducting a thorough analysis of your competitors, you can gain valuable insights that inform your business strategy, highlight unique selling points, and identify areas of opportunity. This section emphasizes the importance of competitor mapping, SWOT analysis, and drawing inspiration from successful biotech startups.

4.1 Competitor Mapping

Identifying Direct Competitors: Research and identify companies that offer similar biotech products or services targeting the same customer segments as your startup.

Analyzing Indirect Competitors: Recognize businesses that may not offer the same products but compete for the same customer dollars or solve similar problems using alternative solutions.

Comparative Analysis: Compare competitors based on factors such as technology, market reach, pricing, regulatory status, and customer satisfaction.

4.2 SWOT Analysis

Strengths: Identify the strengths of your competitors, including their technological expertise, market share, established brand reputation, and successful product lines.

Weaknesses: Evaluate areas where your competitors may be lacking, such as limited geographic presence, gaps in product offerings, or organizational challenges.

Opportunities: Explore potential growth opportunities for your biotech startup based on gaps in the market or untapped customer needs that competitors have not addressed.

Threats: Assess external factors that could pose a threat to your startup's success, such as emerging competitors, changes in regulations, or shifts in market demand.

4.3 Case Study: MediGena Solutions

MediGena Solutions is a promising biotech startup that specializes in therapeutic applications of CRISPR gene editing technology. Through competitor mapping and SWOT analysis, MediGena gained valuable insights to differentiate itself and thrive in the highly competitive gene editing market.

Competitor Mapping for MediGena: MediGena identified direct competitors, including other CRISPR-focused startups, as well as indirect competitors such as gene therapy companies that addressed similar genetic disorders.

SWOT Analysis for MediGena: The analysis revealed that MediGena's key strengths lay in its innovative CRISPR technology, a team of renowned scientists, and strategic partnerships. However, it recognized the need to strengthen its regulatory compliance processes and scale production capabilities.

4.4 Drawing Inspiration from Successful Biotech Startups

Learning from Success Stories: Study successful biotech startups that have overcome challenges and achieved significant milestones. Understand the strategies they employed and how they differentiated themselves from competitors.

Innovation and Uniqueness: Emphasize the importance of innovation and finding a unique value proposition that sets your startup apart from others in the market.

Collaborative Competition: Encourage startups to view competitors not only as rivals but also as potential partners for collaboration and strategic alliances.

4.5 Staying Agile and Adaptable

Continuous Monitoring: Highlight the need to continuously monitor the competitive landscape as it evolves. Market dynamics and competitor strategies can change rapidly in the biotech industry.

Agility in Response: Stress the significance of being agile and adaptable, allowing your startup to pivot and respond quickly to changes in the market and competitive forces.

Leveraging Data and Insights: Emphasize the use of data-driven decision-making and insights gathered from competitor analysis to fine-tune your startup's business model and offerings.

By understanding the competitive landscape through competitor mapping, conducting a comprehensive SWOT analysis, and drawing inspiration from successful biotech startups, readers will be better equipped to craft a robust business strategy and navigate the challenges of the biotechnology market. The case study of MediGena Solutions serves as a practical example of how these analyses can lead to informed decision-making and success in the biotech industry.

Section 5: Leveraging Intellectual Property (IP) and Patents

In the competitive world of biotechnology startups, protecting intellectual property (IP) through patents is crucial. This section delves deeper into the significance of IP protection, the patenting process, and real-world examples of how startups have successfully leveraged their IP portfolios.

1. Importance of Intellectual Property Protection

Innovative ideas and discoveries are the lifeblood of biotech startups. Safeguarding these innovations through IP protection is essential for several reasons:

Market Exclusivity: Patents grant the owner exclusive rights to the invention, preventing competitors from making, using, or selling the same technology, product, or process.

Attracting Investors: A strong IP portfolio can significantly enhance the attractiveness of a biotech startup to investors, as it demonstrates the uniqueness and potential market advantage of the technology.

Commercialization and Licensing Opportunities: Patents allow startups to license their technology to other companies for additional revenue streams and broader market reach.

2. Patent Searches and Freedom-to-Operate Analysis

Before filing a patent application, startups should conduct thorough patent searches to ensure that their inventions are novel and not infringing on existing patents. Additionally, performing freedom-to-operate (FTO) analysis helps identify any existing patents that may pose obstacles to commercialization.

Example: GenoCure Therapeutics

GenoCure Therapeutics, a biotech startup specializing in personalized gene therapies, conducted extensive patent searches and FTO analysis before finalizing their groundbreaking gene editing technology. This ensured that their innovation was unique and could be used without infringing on existing patents, giving them a clear path for commercialization.

3. The Patenting Process

The patenting process can be complex, involving detailed documentation and legal procedures. Startups should consider the following steps:

Patent Drafting: Engage qualified patent attorneys or agents to draft a well-written patent application, describing the invention in a clear and comprehensive manner.

Patent Filing: File the patent application with the appropriate patent office, such as the United States Patent and Trademark Office (USPTO) or the European Patent Office (EPO).

Patent Examination: The patent office examines the application to determine if the invention meets the criteria for patentability, including novelty, non-obviousness, and industrial applicability.

Patent Grant: If the application meets the requirements, the patent office grants the patent, providing the startup with legal protection.

Example: BioGenTech Solutions

BioGenTech Solutions, a startup focusing on cutting-edge genetic diagnostic tools, went through a meticulous patenting process to protect their proprietary testing platform. Their well-drafted patent application successfully secured them a granted patent, allowing them to assert their exclusivity in the market.

4. Building a Strategic IP Portfolio:

Biotech startups should aim to develop a strategic IP portfolio to safeguard multiple aspects of their innovations and maintain a competitive advantage.

Patents on Core Technology: File patents for the central technology that forms the backbone of the startup's products or services.

Continuation Applications: Consider filing continuation applications to cover improvements or additional applications of the original invention.

Trade Secrets and Know-How: Alongside patents, identify trade secrets and know-how that can contribute to the startup's competitive edge and keep them confidential.

Example: NanoBioTech Innovations

NanoBioTech Innovations, a startup specializing in nanomedicine, strategically built an IP portfolio that included patents covering their core nanotechnology, as well as trade secrets related to their unique manufacturing processes. This comprehensive IP approach strengthened their market position and fostered valuable partnerships with pharmaceutical companies.

By effectively leveraging intellectual property rights and following the examples of successful biotech startups, entrepreneurs can protect their innovations and create a solid foundation for future growth and success in the competitive biotechnology industry.

Chapter 5: Building a Strong Biotech Business Plan

1.Elements of a Comprehensive Business Plan

Creating a comprehensive business plan is essential for any biotech startup. This section will break down each element of the plan and provide detailed examples to illustrate their significance in showcasing your biotech venture's potential and viability.

A.Executive Summary

The executive summary is a concise and compelling overview of your entire business plan. It serves as the first impression for potential investors and stakeholders, offering a snapshot of your biotech startup's vision, objectives, and expected outcomes.

Example Executive Summary:

"Our biotech startup, GeneCure Therapeutics, is dedicated to revolutionizing cancer treatment through cutting-edge gene therapies. By targeting specific genetic markers, our personalized therapies have demonstrated promising results in early-stage trials. With a dedicated team of oncology experts and a strong network of research partners, GeneCure Therapeutics aims to deliver hope and healing to cancer patients worldwide."

b) Company Description

The company description provides an in-depth look at your biotech startup's identity, mission, and core values. It presents the story behind your venture, showcasing what sets it apart from others in the industry.

Example Company Description:

"GeneCure Therapeutics was founded by Dr. Emily Roberts, a leading researcher in gene editing technology, driven by a personal mission to enhance cancer patients' quality of life. Our team comprises experienced scientists, oncologists, and business professionals, united by the common goal of eradicating cancer through innovative gene therapies. We firmly believe that by leveraging the potential of biotechnology, we can transform the landscape of cancer treatment and bring hope to countless families affected by this devastating disease."

c) Product or Service Offering

This section details the biotech solution your startup intends to develop and commercialize. Explain the scientific basis, potential applications, and how it addresses critical challenges in the biotech industry or specific fields such as medicine, agriculture, or environmental sustainability.

Example Product or Service Offering:

"GeneCure Therapeutics' flagship product is our proprietary gene editing platform, GeneEditX. Leveraging CRISPR-Cas9 technology, GeneEditX allows precise targeting and modification of genetic sequences associated with various cancer types. Our platform offers a transformative approach to cancer treatment, enabling personalized therapies tailored to each patient's genetic profile. By addressing the root cause of cancer, we aim to provide more effective and less invasive treatment options for patients."

D) Market Analysis

The market analysis section presents a thorough assessment of your target market, potential customers, competitors, and industry trends. Utilize market research data and analysis to substantiate your understanding of the market's needs and opportunities.

Example Market Analysis:

"According to a recent report by GlobalData, the global oncology therapeutics market is projected to reach $200 billion by 2025, driven by the rising incidence of cancer worldwide. GeneCure Therapeutics aims to tap into this rapidly growing market by focusing initially on pediatric leukemia patients with specific genetic markers. Our targeted therapy is positioned to fill a critical gap in the current treatment landscape, offering a highly sought-after solution for patients who have limited treatment options."

e) Marketing and Sales Strategy

Outline your strategies for promoting and selling your biotech product or service. Describe your marketing channels, outreach methods, and sales approaches to reach potential customers, collaborators, and investors.

Example Marketing and Sales Strategy:

"GeneCure Therapeutics will deploy a multi-faceted marketing approach. We will engage in targeted digital advertising campaigns to raise awareness among medical professionals and patient communities. Additionally, we will publish scientific articles in reputable journals to establish credibility and thought leadership in the field. To initiate sales, we will forge strategic partnerships with oncology clinics and hospital networks, allowing us to reach a wider patient base and facilitate clinical trial enrollment."

f) Organizational Structure

Detail the organizational structure of your biotech startup, including key roles and responsibilities of team members. Emphasize how the expertise and experience of your team members contribute to the successful execution of your business plan.

Example Organizational Structure:

"GeneCure Therapeutics boasts a multidisciplinary team of accomplished professionals. Dr. Emily Roberts, our CEO and Chief Scientific Officer, brings over 15 years of experience in gene editing research and has published numerous influential papers in the field. Dr. James Anderson, our Chief Medical Officer, is a renowned oncologist with a proven track record in conducting successful clinical trials. Our business development team, led by Maria Hernandez, possesses extensive experience in forming fruitful collaborations with biotech and pharmaceutical companies."

g) Financial Projections

Financial projections are vital for investors to understand your biotech startup's potential return on investment and growth trajectory. Include revenue forecasts, expense breakdowns, and profit projections over a specific time frame.

Example Financial Projections:

"GeneCure Therapeutics forecasts a conservative revenue of $500,000 for the first year, primarily driven by early-stage partnerships and research grants. We anticipate research and development expenses to account for 60% of our budget, with an additional 25% allocated to marketing and sales efforts. Given our investment in cutting-edge gene editing technology, we expect to break even within the first three years, with exponential growth in revenue following the successful completion of clinical trials and market entry."

Incorporating these elements into your business plan will create a strong foundation for your biotech startup. Remember to keep the language clear and concise while ensuring all aspects are well-researched and supported by data. A compelling business plan can be a crucial factor in attracting potential investors and strategic partners to support your venture.

2. Defining Vision, Mission, and Objectives

In this section, we'll explore the importance of crafting a clear and compelling vision, mission, and specific objectives for your biotech startup. These elements will serve as guiding principles for your team and stakeholders, helping them understand the purpose and direction of your venture.

2.1 Example: Vision for a Biotech Startup

Vision statements express the aspirational and long-term goals of a company. For a biotech startup focused on revolutionizing cancer treatment through gene therapies, the vision might read:

"To revolutionize cancer treatment through cutting-edge gene therapies, providing hope and healing to patients worldwide."

This vision encapsulates the ultimate purpose of the biotech startup, emphasizing its commitment to advancing cancer treatment through innovative and transformative therapies.

2.2 Example: Mission for a Biotech Startup

Mission statements outline the specific actions and activities a company will undertake to achieve its vision. For the same cancer-focused biotech startup, the mission statement could be:

"Our mission is to develop innovative and personalized gene therapies that target cancer at its root cause, significantly improving patient outcomes."

This mission statement conveys the startup's core objective of developing cutting-edge gene therapies with a personalized approach to combat cancer effectively and improve patient outcomes.

2.3 Example: Objectives for the First Year

Setting specific and measurable objectives is crucial for tracking progress and ensuring the startup remains on course. For the biotech startup, the objectives for its first year might include:

Objective 1: Secure seed funding of $1 million to initiate preclinical trials.

Objective 2: Build a strong research team of experts in oncology and gene editing.

Objective 3: Establish partnerships with leading cancer research institutions.

These objectives provide clear milestones for the biotech startup's first year, guiding its efforts toward obtaining funding, assembling a skilled team, and forming strategic collaborations to advance its innovative cancer therapies.

By defining a compelling vision, mission, and specific objectives, the biotech startup can effectively communicate its purpose to potential investors, partners, and employees. Moreover, these guiding statements will serve as a driving force for the team, aligning their efforts and fostering a shared sense of purpose in their pursuit of groundbreaking biotechnology solutions.

3. Strategies for Market Entry and Penetration

Example: Market Entry Strategy

"Initially, focus on pediatric leukemia patients with specific genetic markers, providing a targeted therapy that demonstrates safety and efficacy."

Example: Market Penetration Strategy

"Form alliances with oncology clinics to offer our therapy as a supplemental treatment option, increasing its accessibility to a broader patient base."

4. Financial Projections and Funding Requirements

Example: Financial Projections for a Biotech Startup (Year 1)

Projected Revenue: $500,000 from early-stage partnerships and grants.

Projected Expenses: $800,000, primarily allocated to research, development, and marketing.

Net Loss: ($300,000)

Example: Funding Requirements

"To support our first year of operations and advance preclinical trials, we are seeking $1 million in seed funding from angel investors and strategic partners."

5. Crafting a Solid Marketing and Sales Plan

Example: Marketing Plan

"Our marketing efforts will include targeted online advertising, content marketing to engage with medical professionals and patients, and attending key industry conferences."

Example: Sales Plan

"We will initially engage directly with oncology clinics and hospitals to introduce our therapy and build relationships with key decision-makers."

This chapter aims to provide you with practical examples to assist in creating a compelling biotech business plan that aligns with your startup's vision and goals. Remember, your business plan should be dynamic and adaptable to changes as your biotech venture progresses.

Chapter 6: Funding and Investment Strategies

In the fast-paced world of biotechnology startups, securing adequate funding is a critical step on the path to success. Turning groundbreaking ideas into tangible products or therapies requires significant financial resources, and biotech entrepreneurs must navigate various funding options to fuel their ventures. In this chapter, we explore the diverse funding and investment strategies available to biotech startups, along with real-world examples of successful funding journeys.

1. Funding Options for Biotech Startups:

1.1. Angel Investors:

Angel investors are high-net-worth individuals who invest their personal capital in early-stage startups, often providing mentorship and expertise along with funding. These investors are typically passionate about the life sciences and eager to support innovative biotech ventures. For instance, in the early 2000s, angel investor Ron Conway played a pivotal role in funding companies like Google and Facebook. Similarly, in the biotech sector, investor and entrepreneur Peter Thiel's support helped launch several successful startups, including Moderna, a groundbreaking mRNA therapeutics company.

1.2. Venture Capital (VC):

Venture capital firms invest in startups with high growth potential in exchange for equity. VCs often fund companies in later stages compared to angel investors, but they can provide larger sums of capital to fuel rapid expansion. A noteworthy example is Flagship Pioneering, a venture capital firm that has backed numerous biotech startups, such as Seres Therapeutics and Moderna, helping them reach valuation milestones and commercial success.

1.3. Government Grants and Research Funding:

Many governments offer grants and funding programs to support biotechnology research and development. These grants not only provide financial support but also lend credibility to the startup's technology. The U.S. National Institutes of Health (NIH) and the European Union's Horizon Europe program are prominent sources of government funding for biotech research. For example, CRISPR Therapeutics, a gene-editing pioneer, received early funding from government grants before attracting significant private investment.

2. Pitching to Investors: Dos and Don'ts:

2.1. Do: Thoroughly Prepare and Tailor Your Pitch:

Before approaching investors, conduct extensive research on their investment focus and portfolio. Tailor your pitch to align with their interests and highlight the unique value proposition of your biotech startup. Present a clear and compelling vision of your product or therapy's potential impact on the market and society.

2.2. Don't: Overpromise or Misrepresent:

While it's essential to be enthusiastic about your startup's potential, avoid making unrealistic promises or misrepresenting data. Investors value transparency and due diligence. Be honest about the challenges your startup may face and the potential risks involved.

3. Navigating the Due Diligence Process:

3.1. Preparing for Due Diligence:

Expect potential investors to conduct a thorough due diligence process to assess your startup's viability and potential risks. Organize all relevant documentation, including intellectual property, financial statements, and regulatory approvals, to expedite the process and demonstrate your startup's professionalism.

3.2. Building Trust and Credibility:

Transparency and responsiveness are crucial during due diligence. Address any inquiries promptly and honestly, as this builds trust with investors and showcases your commitment to success.

4. Real-world Examples:

4.1. Moderna Therapeutics:

Moderna, a pioneer in mRNA therapeutics, experienced a successful funding journey. The company received early support from angel investors and venture capital firms like Flagship Pioneering. Government grants, including funding from the Defense Advanced Research Projects Agency (DARPA), played a significant role in advancing their mRNA vaccine technology. Moderna's successful IPO in 2018 marked a significant milestone in its funding trajectory, further strengthening its financial position.

4.2. Editas Medicine:

Editas Medicine, a leading gene-editing company, secured funding from a diverse range of investors. Notable investors included the Bill & Melinda Gates Foundation and Google Ventures (GV), which recognized the potential of CRISPR/Cas9 gene-editing technology. Editas Medicine's IPO in 2016 demonstrated investor confidence in its groundbreaking gene-editing platform.

In conclusion, funding is the lifeblood of biotechnology startups, and entrepreneurs must strategically navigate various funding options to turn their visions into reality. By understanding the available funding sources, tailoring their pitches, and diligently navigating the due diligence process, biotech entrepreneurs can secure the financial backing needed to drive innovation and make a lasting impact on healthcare, agriculture, and the environment. The examples of successful biotech startups mentioned above illustrate how strategic funding decisions can shape the trajectory of a startup, paving the way for transformative breakthroughs in biotechnology.

Chapter 7: Legal and Regulatory Considerations for Biotech Startups

In the world of biotechnology, the potential for groundbreaking innovations is immense. As a biotech entrepreneur, you are driven by a passion to make a positive impact on society and revolutionize various industries. However, along with these aspirations come significant legal and regulatory challenges that can make or break your startup. This chapter will delve into the critical legal and regulatory considerations that biotech startups must navigate, with real-life examples to illustrate their importance.

1.Understanding Biotech Regulations: The FDA and Beyond

Biotechnology products often fall under the purview of strict regulatory bodies like the U.S. Food and Drug Administration (FDA) or its equivalent in other countries. These regulations are in place to ensure safety, efficacy, and ethical standards are met before products are introduced to the market. Compliance with such regulations is crucial for the success of a biotech startup.

Example 1: FDA Approval for a Novel Medical Device

Consider a biotech startup working on a novel medical device for monitoring blood glucose levels in diabetic patients. To bring this device to market, the startup needs to adhere to the FDA's rigorous approval process for medical devices. This involves conducting extensive preclinical studies, clinical trials, and submitting detailed documentation to demonstrate the device's safety and efficacy. The process can be time-consuming and costly, but obtaining FDA clearance will be essential for gaining trust from healthcare providers and potential investors.

Intellectual Property Protection and Licensing

Protecting intellectual property (IP) is paramount in the highly competitive biotech industry. Patents, trademarks, and copyrights safeguard your novel discoveries and prevent others from copying or using your innovations without permission. Additionally, licensing agreements can be a strategic way for biotech startups to leverage their IP and collaborate with larger companies.

Example 2: Patenting a Gene Editing Technology

Imagine a biotech startup that has developed a revolutionary gene-editing technology with vast applications in various industries. By filing for patents to protect this technology, the startup can prevent competitors from replicating its breakthrough process. Furthermore, the startup can explore licensing agreements with pharmaceutical companies or agricultural firms to use the technology in drug development or crop improvement, generating both revenue and strategic partnerships.

FDA and Other Regulatory Approvals

For startups developing biopharmaceuticals or other biologics, obtaining regulatory approvals is a significant milestone. These approvals not only allow products to enter the market but also establish credibility and trust among potential customers, investors, and partners.

Example 3: Obtaining FDA Approval for a Novel Drug

Suppose a biotech startup is working on a groundbreaking gene therapy to treat a rare genetic disorder. The path to FDA approval involves rigorous testing in preclinical and clinical trials to ensure safety and efficacy. Despite the challenges and costs involved, gaining FDA approval can be transformative for the startup, as it opens up opportunities for collaboration with established pharmaceutical companies, access to larger markets, and potentially life-changing treatment options for patients.

Compliance and Risk Management

Biotech startups must navigate a complex web of compliance requirements, from data privacy and patient confidentiality to ethical considerations regarding research involving human subjects. Effective risk management practices are vital to ensure the startup operates within legal boundaries and minimizes potential liabilities.

Example 4: Ethical Considerations in Biotech Research

Suppose a biotech startup is working on a project that involves gene editing in human embryos to correct genetic defects. While this technology holds immense potential for preventing hereditary diseases, it raises ethical questions about the potential misuse or unforeseen consequences. Proper risk management and adherence to ethical guidelines are essential to address these concerns responsibly and gain support from the scientific community and regulatory bodies.

International Regulations and Market Access

For biotech startups aiming to expand globally, understanding international regulations is crucial. Each country may have its own unique requirements for the import, export, and distribution of biotech products.

Example 5: Global Distribution of a Diagnostic Test

Consider a biotech startup that has developed a diagnostic test for detecting a prevalent infectious disease. To enter international markets, the startup must navigate various regulatory processes and obtain approvals from each country's relevant health authorities. Additionally, the startup needs to consider potential cultural and regional differences that could affect the acceptance and adoption of the test.

Conclusion :

Navigating the legal and regulatory landscape is a fundamental aspect of the biotech startup journey. The examples discussed in this chapter illustrate the real-world challenges and opportunities that arise in the pursuit of bringing biotechnological innovations to market. As a bio-innovator, understanding and proactively addressing these considerations will not only ensure compliance but also bolster your startup's credibility, foster strategic partnerships, and ultimately lead to a more successful and impactful biotech venture. Embrace these challenges as an opportunity to shape the future of biotechnology responsibly and ethically, making a lasting difference in the lives of people and the world at large.

Chapter 8: Assembling the Right Team

Introduction

In the fast-paced world of biotechnology startups, having the right team can make all the difference between success and failure. Assembling a team of dedicated, skilled, and passionate individuals is essential for tackling the complex challenges that come with launching a biotech venture. In this chapter, we will explore the critical aspects of team-building for biotech startups, including identifying key team roles, recruiting top talent, fostering collaboration, and building a culture of innovation.

1.Identifying Key Team Roles and Skillsets

Building a biotech startup team requires careful consideration of the specific skill sets and roles needed to drive the company's mission forward. Depending on the nature of the startup idea, certain roles become particularly vital:

Scientific Experts: Biotech ventures often revolve around cutting-edge research and technological innovation. Scientists and researchers with expertise in relevant domains like molecular biology, genetics, pharmacology, or bioinformatics play a crucial role in shaping the startup's core technology.

Business and Management Leaders: Beyond scientific expertise, biotech startups require strong business acumen. Visionary leaders with experience in business development, finance, and project management can steer the company towards growth and profitability.

Regulatory and Compliance Specialists: As biotech products and services undergo strict regulatory scrutiny, having experts in navigating complex regulatory landscapes ensures compliance and minimizes risks.

Product Development and Engineering Professionals: Biotech startups that create tangible products or devices necessitate skilled engineers and product developers who can translate scientific concepts into functional prototypes.

Marketing and Sales Professionals: An effective marketing and sales team are essential for gaining traction in the market and securing strategic partnerships or collaborations.

Recruiting and Retaining Top Talent

The process of recruiting top talent for a biotech startup is both exciting and challenging. Here are some strategies to attract and retain the best team members:

Cultivate a Compelling Vision: Talented individuals are drawn to startups with a clear and compelling vision. Communicate the startup's mission and the potential impact it can have on society to ignite passion and commitment.

Offer Equity and Incentives: Biotech startups often have limited resources, making it challenging to offer competitive salaries. Providing equity or stock options can be an attractive incentive for potential team members who believe in the long-term success of the venture.

Networking and Partnerships: Leverage industry connections and academic networks to identify potential team members. Collaborating with research institutions can be an excellent way to access top-notch researchers and scientists.

Create a Positive Work Environment: A positive and supportive work environment fosters creativity and productivity. Promote a culture of open communication, where team members feel valued and encouraged to share their ideas.

Emphasize Career Growth and Learning Opportunities: Highlight the learning and growth opportunities that come with working in a startup. Offering training programs or opportunities for further education can attract ambitious individuals looking to expand their skill set.

Building an Effective Interdisciplinary Team

Biotech startups require diverse skill sets and expertise, making interdisciplinary collaboration crucial. Successful teams blend scientific expertise with business acumen and engineering prowess:

Facilitate Collaboration Across Disciplines: Encourage regular meetings and open discussions between team members from different backgrounds. Creating a sense of camaraderie and mutual respect fosters a collaborative atmosphere.

Promote Knowledge Sharing: Establish mechanisms for sharing knowledge and insights across the team. Whether through regular presentations, workshops, or shared documentation, keeping everyone informed and engaged is key.

Cross-functional Projects: Assigning team members to cross-functional projects allows individuals to explore new areas and learn from their peers. This interdisciplinary approach enhances problem-solving and creativity.

The Role of Advisors and Mentors

Having experienced advisors and mentors can significantly impact the success of a biotech startup:

Advisory Board Formation: Consider establishing an advisory board comprising seasoned industry experts, entrepreneurs, and academics. Their guidance can help steer the startup towards the right direction and provide valuable insights.

Mentorship Programs: Encourage team members to seek mentorship from seasoned professionals. Mentorship relationships offer a wealth of knowledge, connections, and career guidance.

Fostering a Culture of Innovation and Collaboration

Building a culture that embraces innovation and collaboration is fundamental for biotech startups:

Risk-taking and Learning from Failure: Encourage calculated risk-taking and view failures as opportunities for learning and growth. A culture that doesn't penalize failure fosters an environment where creative thinking thrives.

Supporting Research and Development: Allocate resources and time for research and development efforts. Invest in cutting-edge technologies and infrastructure that empower scientists and researchers to explore new frontiers.

Innovation Workshops and Hackathons: Organize innovation workshops and hackathons to stimulate creativity and cross-pollinate ideas within the team.

Conclusion

Assembling the right team is the backbone of any successful biotech startup. By identifying key roles, recruiting top talent, fostering collaboration, and building a culture of innovation, entrepreneurs can set the stage for groundbreaking achievements. In this chapter, we have explored various strategies to attract and retain top-notch talent, as well as the importance of interdisciplinary collaboration and mentorship. Building a strong team is not only crucial for immediate success but also paves the way for long-term growth and impact within the biotechnology industry.

Examples of Successful Biotech Startup Teams

1. CRISPR Therapeutics AG:

CRISPR Therapeutics, a leading biotech company in gene editing, was founded by Emmanuelle Charpentier, Jennifer Doudna, and their colleagues. Emmanuelle and Jennifer's expertise in CRISPR-Cas9 technology laid the foundation for the startup. They recruited a team of scientists, bioinformaticians, and business leaders to advance their gene editing platform. With a focus on collaboration and innovative research, CRISPR Therapeutics achieved significant milestones in developing potential cures for genetic disorders.

Moderna, Inc.:

Moderna, a pioneer in messenger RNA (mRNA) therapeutics, was co-founded by Derrick Rossi and a team of leading scientists and biotech entrepreneurs. The team included scientists with expertise in mRNA technology, drug development, and immunology. The startup's interdisciplinary approach and strategic partnerships with academic institutions and pharmaceutical companies propelled Moderna's success in developing mRNA-based vaccines and therapies.

GRAIL, Inc.:

GRAIL, a biotech startup focused on early cancer detection, was founded by a group of industry experts, including Jeff Huber, George Golumbeski, and others. The company brought together researchers, clinicians, and data scientists to develop a multi-cancer early detection test using advanced genomic sequencing and machine learning algorithms. The diverse expertise of the team was instrumental in advancing GRAIL's pioneering liquid biopsy technology.

These examples illustrate how a combination of visionary founders, a diverse and skilled team, and a supportive work culture can lead to transformative breakthroughs in biotechnology startups. The success of these startups highlights the significance of assembling the right team as the foundation for innovation and impact in the biotech industry.

Chapter 9: Funding and Scaling the Biotech Startup

In Chapter 9, we delve into the crucial phase of funding and scaling for biotech startups. This phase marks a significant turning point in the life of a biotech venture, where successful execution can lead to rapid growth and expansion, while missteps can hinder progress or even lead to failure. We explore various funding options, strategies for scaling, forming strategic partnerships, and the challenges and opportunities that come with expanding a biotech startup. Throughout the chapter, we present real-world examples and case studies to illustrate the concepts and lessons discussed.

Section 1: Bootstrapping and Early-Stage Funding

In this section, we examine the early stages of a biotech startup's journey, when founders often rely on personal savings, friends and family investments, or bootstrapping to get their projects off the ground. Bootstrapping is a common approach for startups in their infancy, as it allows them to retain full control over their ventures and test their ideas without diluting equity.

However, bootstrapping has its limitations, as funding is often limited, and progress can be slow. Founders must be scrappy and resourceful, making every penny count. They must prioritize critical aspects, such as research and development, and find cost-effective solutions for tasks like marketing and administration.

Example:

Case Study: "GeneTech Diagnostics"

"GeneTech Diagnostics" was founded by a team of young scientists with a vision to revolutionize early cancer detection using innovative genetic screening technology. With limited external funding, they pooled their personal savings and secured a small seed grant from a research foundation. Through prudent financial planning and relentless dedication, they successfully developed a prototype and conducted preliminary clinical trials. Their early achievements attracted the attention of angel investors and venture capitalists, leading to substantial Series A funding and propelling them into the next phase of scaling.

The founders of "GeneTech Diagnostics" had to make tough decisions regarding where to allocate their limited funds. They invested heavily in cutting-edge laboratory equipment, which was essential for conducting their research. To save costs on office space, they started the company in a small shared laboratory, demonstrating their commitment and vision to potential investors.

This case study illustrates the importance of resourcefulness and perseverance during the bootstrapping phase. Founders must be prepared to wear multiple hats and navigate challenges creatively to lay a strong foundation for future growth.

Section 2: Scaling the Startup: Challenges and Strategies

Scaling a biotech startup requires careful planning and execution. This section explores the challenges entrepreneurs face as they transition from proof-of-concept to large-scale production and commercialization. Rapid growth brings a new set of complexities, including increased demand for products or services, manufacturing and logistical challenges, and maintaining product quality and consistency.

One of the significant challenges in scaling biotech startups is securing sufficient funding to support expansion. Startups need to attract larger investments to build infrastructure, hire additional staff, and conduct larger clinical trials or studies.

Moreover, regulatory compliance becomes more stringent as the startup's product or service reaches a larger audience. Ensuring compliance with local and international regulations is critical for successful scaling. Additionally, startups must focus on recruiting top talent to support their expansion. Hiring skilled professionals who align with the company's mission and culture becomes paramount.

Example:

Case Study: "GreenAgri Biotech"

"GreenAgri Biotech" developed a groundbreaking plant biotechnology solution that enhanced crop yields while minimizing the need for chemical fertilizers. As demand for their product grew, they faced challenges in meeting the market's needs at scale. The company realized that to achieve substantial growth, they needed to scale their manufacturing capabilities significantly.

To address this challenge, "GreenAgri Biotech" took a phased approach to scale their production. Initially, they invested in optimizing their existing production processes and implementing automation to increase efficiency. As they gained traction in the market, they secured additional funding from venture capital firms to establish a state-of-the-art manufacturing facility.

During this scaling phase, the company faced unforeseen supply chain challenges due to fluctuations in raw material availability. To mitigate these risks, they strategically partnered with suppliers and established long-term contracts, ensuring a stable supply of essential resources.

To ensure product quality and consistency, "GreenAgri Biotech" implemented stringent quality control measures and conducted extensive testing throughout the manufacturing process. They obtained certifications that demonstrated their commitment to maintaining the highest standards, earning the trust of farmers and agricultural distributors.

Through their carefully planned scaling strategy, "GreenAgri Biotech" successfully met the growing demand for their product, expanding their market reach both nationally and internationally.

This case study highlights the importance of meticulous planning and adaptability in the scaling process. Scaling requires constant evaluation and adjustment to overcome unforeseen challenges while maintaining product integrity and customer satisfaction.

Section 3: Strategic Partnerships and Collaborations

Forming strategic partnerships and collaborations can be instrumental in the success of a biotech startup. In this section, we explore the various types of partnerships, such as academic-industry collaborations, research collaborations, and licensing agreements. We discuss how these alliances can accelerate research and development, provide access to specialized expertise, and facilitate regulatory approvals.

Collaborating with academic institutions allows biotech startups to tap into cutting-edge research and gain access to a pool of talented researchers and scientists. Universities, on the other hand, benefit from industrial collaboration by seeing their research translated into practical applications.

Example:

Case Study: "PharmaBio Therapeutics"

"PharmaBio Therapeutics" was a biotech startup focused on developing novel therapeutics for rare diseases. Recognizing the need for specialized clinical expertise, they formed a strategic partnership with a prominent research hospital. This collaboration not only accelerated their clinical trials but also bolstered their credibility in the industry. As a result,

"PharmaBio Therapeutics" attracted significant venture capital investment, paving the way for further expansion and the eventual launch of their first FDA-approved therapy.

The collaboration between "PharmaBio Therapeutics" and the research hospital allowed them to access a vast network of patients, crucial for conducting clinical trials for their rare disease therapies. The hospital's experienced clinical research team and state-of-the-art facilities ensured rigorous and efficient trials. As a result, "PharmaBio Therapeutics" was able to progress through the clinical development stages faster than if they had operated independently.

Moreover, the partnership enhanced the startup's reputation and credibility, as it demonstrated that established medical professionals recognized the potential of their therapies. This increased investor confidence and attracted the attention of venture capital firms seeking promising opportunities in the biotech space.

This case study illustrates how strategic collaborations can provide startups with a competitive edge, facilitate access to crucial resources, and accelerate their journey to market-readiness.

Section 4: Expanding Internationally: Opportunities and Pitfalls

As biotech startups achieve success in their domestic markets, the allure of international expansion becomes evident. However, entering foreign markets involves navigating unique regulatory landscapes, cultural differences, and competitive challenges. This section explores the opportunities and potential pitfalls of global expansion and provides guidance on effective international market entry strategies.

Expanding internationally presents startups with access to broader customer bases and diverse markets. It can also be a strategic move to mitigate risks by reducing dependence on a single market. However, entering new territories requires comprehensive market research, understanding local regulations, and adapting products or services to meet cultural preferences and specific needs.

Example:

Case Study: "MediGen Solutions"

"MediGen Solutions" developed innovative medical devices with broad applications in the healthcare industry. After establishing a strong presence in their home country,

They explored international markets for growth. However, they faced regulatory hurdles and certification requirements in each new market. To overcome these challenges, they partnered with local distributors who had established networks and expertise in navigating the regulatory landscape. These partnerships facilitated "MediGen Solutions" successful entry into multiple countries, significantly expanding their market share.

The founders of "MediGen Solutions" recognized that a one-size-fits-all approach to international expansion would not work. Each country had its own regulatory authorities, standards, and certification requirements for medical devices. To expedite the approval process, they formed strategic partnerships with local distributors who had in-depth knowledge of the local healthcare market and strong relationships with regulatory bodies.

These partnerships allowed "MediGen Solutions" to navigate the complexities of international regulations efficiently. The distributors helped with product registrations, certifications, and marketing strategies tailored to each specific region. By collaborating with local experts, "MediGen Solutions" overcame regulatory hurdles and quickly gained market access, achieving significant market penetration in various countries.

This case study illustrates the importance of understanding and adapting to local regulations and cultural nuances when expanding internationally. Strategic partnerships with experienced local players can be instrumental in successfully entering new markets.

Section 5: Case Studies of Successful Scaling in Biotech Startups

In this concluding section, we present additional case studies of biotech startups that successfully scaled their operations and achieved significant milestones. We examine the strategies they employed, the challenges they overcame, and the lessons learned from their journeys.

Examples:

1. "NanoCure Therapeutics": A startup focused on nanotechnology-based drug delivery systems that tackled scaling challenges by establishing a state-of-the-art manufacturing facility and securing strategic partnerships with pharmaceutical companies.

2. "BioGrow AgriTech": An agricultural biotech startup that scaled its operations globally by licensing its technology to regional partners and adapting its solutions to diverse agricultural ecosystems.

In conclusion, Chapter 9 of "Bio-Innovators' Blueprint: Startup Ideas in Biotechnology" delves into the critical phase of funding and scaling for biotech startups. This phase marks a significant turning point in a biotech venture's journey, where successful execution can lead to rapid growth and expansion, while missteps can hinder progress or even lead to failure. Throughout the chapter, we have explored various funding options, strategies for scaling, forming strategic partnerships, and the challenges and opportunities that come with expanding a biotech startup.

The early-stage funding phase is characterized by bootstrapping, where founders leverage personal savings, friends and family investments, or creative cost-saving measures to bring their ideas to life. The case study of "GeneTech Diagnostics" showcased the resourcefulness and perseverance required during this phase, emphasizing the importance of careful financial planning and strategic allocation of limited resources.

As a biotech startup progresses and achieves proof-of-concept, the scaling phase presents new challenges and complexities. "GreenAgri Biotech's" case study illustrated the need for careful planning, the establishment of scalable infrastructure, and efficient supply chain management to meet growing market demand. Successful scaling requires continuous evaluation, adaptability, and a commitment to maintaining product quality and customer satisfaction.

Strategic partnerships and collaborations are instrumental in accelerating research and development, accessing specialized expertise, and navigating complex regulatory landscapes. The case study of "PharmaBio Therapeutics" demonstrated the significant impact of forming a strategic partnership with a research hospital, which not only accelerated their clinical trials but also enhanced their credibility and attracted further funding.

Expanding internationally offers startups access to broader markets and diversification, but it also comes with regulatory and cultural challenges. The case study of "MediGen Solutions" highlighted the importance of forming partnerships with local distributors to overcome regulatory hurdles and achieve successful market entry in multiple countries.

The chapter's concluding section presented additional case studies of successful scaling in biotech startups, such as "NanoCure Therapeutics" and "BioGrow AgriTech." These examples showcased diverse strategies and approaches to scaling, emphasizing the importance of tailoring strategies to each startup's unique needs and industry segment.

In summary, funding and scaling are pivotal phases in the entrepreneurial journey of biotech startups. Navigating these phases successfully requires a combination of visionary leadership, strategic planning, adaptability, and an unwavering commitment to excellence. The lessons learned from real-world case studies provide invaluable insights and inspiration for aspiring bio-entrepreneurs as they embark on their own biotech startup ventures. The journey from idea conception to market success is challenging, but with the right strategies, partnerships, and perseverance, biotech startups have the potential to make a significant impact on society, advancing healthcare, agriculture, sustainability, and more. As the biotech industry continues to evolve, the Bio-Innovators' Blueprint aims to equip entrepreneurs with the knowledge and tools they need to thrive in this dynamic and transformative field.

Chapter 10: Exit Strategies and Future Trends

Introduction:

Chapter 10 explores the critical phase of scaling a biotech startup. As entrepreneurs witness their ventures grow, they face the crucial decision of planning their exit strategies, evaluating options such as acquisitions or initial public offerings (IPOs), and preparing for the path that lies ahead. This chapter also delves into emerging trends in biotech entrepreneurship, showcasing the pioneers who are shaping the future of the industry.

Section 1: Evaluating Exit Options

Acquisition Allure:

Acquisition is often an appealing exit strategy for biotech startups. When established biotech companies or larger corporations acquire innovative startups, they gain access to cutting-edge technology, intellectual property, and skilled talent. An acquisition can provide a lucrative exit for the startup's founders and investors. For example, in the pharmaceutical sector, big pharma companies often acquire smaller biotech startups to bolster their drug pipelines and expand their market presence. One notable example is the acquisition of Kite Pharma by Gilead Sciences, which propelled Gilead's entry into the promising field of CAR-T cell therapy.

Paving the IPO Path:

Going public through an IPO offers biotech startups access to substantial capital and increased visibility in the market. While the IPO process can be challenging, it provides an opportunity for the general public and institutional investors to participate in the company's growth. Notable success stories include the IPOs of Moderna and BioNTech, which garnered significant attention due to their pioneering mRNA-based vaccine technologies. These IPOs not only brought substantial funding to the companies but also elevated their profiles as leaders in vaccine development.

Section 2: Preparing for Exit

2.1 Fine-tuning the Business:

Before pursuing an exit, biotech startups must focus on fine-tuning their business operations and maximizing their value.

This involves establishing a strong leadership team capable of executing the company's vision. An efficient operational structure, well-documented processes, and robust supply chain management are essential to appeal to potential acquirers or investors. For instance, during its scaling phase, the biotech startup Grail invested heavily in building a strong team of scientists and professionals, which played a crucial role in its eventual acquisition by Illumina.

2.2 Navigating Negotiations:

Exit negotiations require careful handling to strike the right balance between securing favorable terms for the founders and investors while maintaining the integrity of the company. In some cases, startups may need to negotiate earn-outs or performance-based agreements to align the interests of all parties involved. For example, when the biotech company Juno Therapeutics was acquired by Celgene, negotiations involved considerations such as clinical trial progress, regulatory approvals, and potential milestones to determine the final acquisition price.

Section 3: Life After Exit

3.1 Lessons from Biotech Entrepreneurs:

Post-exit, biotech entrepreneurs often find themselves with newfound resources and opportunities. Some choose to invest in other startups or venture capital funds, leveraging their expertise to support the next generation of innovators. Others may explore new entrepreneurial ventures or join established companies to continue making an impact in the industry. A prime example is the founder of Sage Therapeutics, who, after the successful acquisition of Sage by Biogen, went on to invest in promising biotech startups focused on neurological disorders.

3.2 Exploring New Ventures:

Entrepreneurs who have exited successful biotech startups may venture into new areas, leveraging their experiences to address emerging challenges or unmet needs. Their expertise and network can open doors to innovative collaborations and partnerships. For instance, the co-founders of 23andMe, after the company's IPO, began exploring other healthcare-related opportunities, including drug discovery and development.

Section 4: Predicting the Future of Biotechnology Startups

4.1 Beyond Traditional Biotech:

As the biotech industry evolves, it converges with other cutting-edge technologies such as artificial intelligence (AI), blockchain, and nanotechnology. Startups exploring these convergent technologies are at the forefront of shaping the future of biotech. For instance, AI-driven drug discovery platforms are accelerating the identification of potential therapeutic targets, significantly shortening the drug development timeline.

4.2 Personalized Medicine and Beyond:

The future of biotech lies in personalized medicine, where treatments are tailored to individual patients based on their genetic makeup, lifestyle, and other factors. With advancements in genomics and data analytics, startups are developing personalized therapies for various diseases, offering targeted and more effective treatments. Additionally, biotech startups are increasingly focusing on sustainability and environmentally-friendly solutions, such as bio-based materials and renewable energy sources.

Conclusion:

Chapter 10 paints a vivid picture of the scaling phase in biotech entrepreneurship, where exit strategies and future trends play a pivotal role. Entrepreneurs are encouraged to carefully evaluate their exit options, prepare diligently for the next chapter, and embrace the exciting possibilities that lie ahead.

As the biotech industry continues to evolve, pioneers in the field are forging new paths, ushering in a future where innovation and entrepreneurship converge to address global challenges and improve lives worldwide.

Bio-Innovators Unleashed: Embracing the Entrepreneurial Journey in Biotechnology

Chapter 11: Conclusion: Your Journey Begins

In this concluding chapter, we embark on a transformative journey, celebrating the culmination of our exploration into the world of biotech entrepreneurship. We've dived deep into the realms of innovative biotech startup ideas, market dynamics, funding strategies, and ethical considerations. Now, it's time to channel our inspiration into action and take the first steps towards becoming bio-innovators.

Section 1: Recap of Key Takeaways

We begin by revisiting the core lessons learned throughout this book. From understanding biotechnology trends to crafting robust business plans, we'll recapitulate the essential knowledge necessary to kickstart your biotech venture. Remember, each piece of wisdom forms a critical building block of your entrepreneurial success.

Section 2: Embracing the Role of a Bio-Innovator

The path of a bio-innovator is one of passion, dedication, and perseverance. We'll delve into the mindset and qualities that distinguish successful biotech entrepreneurs. Drawing insights from established leaders in the biotech industry, we'll explore the traits that empower these visionaries to overcome challenges and drive meaningful change.

Example: Angela's Journey

Meet Angela, a determined bio-innovator who founded a startup aiming to revolutionize cancer diagnostics. We'll follow Angela's story, from her initial idea to her triumphs and setbacks, illustrating the tenacity required to navigate the unpredictable biotech landscape.

Section 3: Encouragement and Inspiration for Future Bio-Entrepreneurs

The road to biotech entrepreneurship may be daunting, but it is also full of limitless possibilities. In this section, we'll draw inspiration from the successes of iconic biotech startups and individuals who overcame adversity to make a significant impact. Their stories will ignite your passion and fuel your drive to pursue your dreams fearlessly.

Example: Beyond Boundaries

Explore the tale of a group of young researchers who harnessed the power of gene-editing technology to create affordable solutions for genetic disorders in low-income communities. Their boundary-pushing approach exemplifies the transformative potential of biotechnology for social good.

Section 4: Resources for Further Exploration

Knowledge is power, and in the world of biotech entrepreneurship, continuous learning is key. We'll provide an extensive list of resources, including recommended books, academic journals, industry publications, and online platforms, to empower you with an arsenal of information for your ongoing journey.

Example: Learning Beyond the Book

Meet Kevin, an avid learner and bio-entrepreneur, who shares his experiences with self-education and how he leveraged online courses, webinars, and networking events to stay ahead in the rapidly evolving biotech landscape.

Section 5: Acknowledgments

The journey of writing this book would not have been possible without the collective support, inspiration, and collaboration of numerous individuals and organizations. In this section, we express gratitude to those who have contributed to the creation of "Bio-Innovators Unleashed."

Example: A Grateful Heart

We acknowledge the invaluable insights shared by leading biotech researchers, entrepreneurs, and industry experts during our quest to explore the realm of biotech startups. Their wisdom has enriched this book and will undoubtedly inspire countless future bio-innovators.

Conclusion: Pioneering the Future of Biotech Entrepreneurship

Congratulations, dear reader, on reaching the final chapter of "Bio-Innovators Unleashed: Embracing the Entrepreneurial Journey in Biotechnology." We have embarked on an extraordinary voyage, exploring the boundless potential of biotech startups and discovering the essential ingredients for success in this dynamic realm. As you close this book, we want to leave you not only with a sense of accomplishment but also with the tools and mindset to propel your aspirations forward.

Throughout this journey, we have witnessed the transformative power of biotechnology, as it continues to revolutionize industries and redefine human well-being. Each chapter has illuminated a unique facet of biotech entrepreneurship, guiding you from ideation to market entry, scaling, and beyond. As we part ways, we want to impart some final reflections and author's tips to invigorate your path ahead.

1.Embrace the Power of Innovation

At the heart of biotech entrepreneurship lies the pursuit of innovative solutions to pressing challenges. Unleash your creativity, challenge conventions, and dare to dream big. Break free from the confines of the ordinary and venture into uncharted territories, for therein lies the potential for true impact.

Persistence Fuels Progress

Building a biotech startup is not without hurdles. Embrace failures as stepping stones to success. Keep learning, iterating, and refining your approach. The journey of an entrepreneur is often filled with setbacks, but it is the unwavering determination that separates those who thrive from those who merely survive.

Seek Collaboration and Mentorship

No one succeeds alone. Forge meaningful partnerships, collaborate with experts, and surround yourself with a diverse team. Seek out mentors who can provide guidance, wisdom, and a fresh perspective. Together, you will overcome obstacles and elevate your startup to greater heights.

Impact with Purpose

Biotechnology wields immense power, capable of shaping the future of humanity. As a bio-innovator, recognize the responsibility that comes with this potential. Strive to create solutions that benefit society, advance sustainability, and improve lives. Let purpose guide your entrepreneurial journey.

Adapt to Change

In the rapidly evolving biotech landscape, adaptability is the key to survival. Stay attuned to emerging trends, technologies, and market shifts. Be willing to pivot and embrace change, for therein lie opportunities for exponential growth.

Foster a Culture of Resilience

As you build your startup, foster a culture that celebrates resilience and embraces risk-taking. Encourage open communication, collaboration, and a willingness to experiment. In this dynamic environment, innovation flourishes, and breakthroughs are born.

Balance Ambition with Realism

Set ambitious goals, but temper them with pragmatism. Understand the scope of your resources and the timeline for execution. Strike a balance between aspirational vision and realistic planning to sustainably drive your venture forward.

Cultivate a Continuous Learning Mindset

Never stop learning. The biotech landscape is ever-changing, and staying relevant requires a commitment to continuous education. Remain curious, seek knowledge, and be open to insights from diverse sources.

As you step beyond the pages of this book and embark on your own biotech entrepreneurial journey, remember that the world needs visionary bio-innovators like you. The challenges we face as a global community demand bold solutions and audacious thinkers. You have the power to shape the future, disrupt industries, and elevate the human experience.

In the face of uncertainty, remember the words of Robert F. Kennedy: **"Only those who dare to fail greatly can ever achieve greatly."** Embrace failure as a stepping stone toward greatness and resilience. As you move forward, let passion, purpose, and perseverance be your guiding lights.

The path'you've chosen may be arduous, but the potential for impact is immeasurable. You have the opportunity to leave a lasting legacy, shaping the course of human progress through biotech entrepreneurship. So, go forth with courage, tenacity, and an unwavering commitment to making a difference.

Thank you for joining us on this exploration of biotech entrepreneurship. We have every confidence that you will not only pioneer the future of biotechnology but also inspire countless others to join the ranks of bio-innovators, propelling the world toward a brighter, healthier, and more sustainable tomorrow.

With heartfelt wishes for your success,

[Ramatenki Saye Ddarshanu]

Author of "Bio-Innovators' Blueprint: Startup Ideas in Biotechnology"

Bonus: 50 Innovative Ideas for New Startups in Biotechnology

As a token of appreciation for your support and dedication to the world of biotechnology entrepreneurship, we are delighted to present you with a special bonus section. Within these pages, you will find 50 innovative startup ideas that have the potential to disrupt industries, revolutionize healthcare, and contribute to a sustainable future. Each idea is a seed of possibility, waiting for visionary bio-innovators like you to nurture and cultivate into transformative ventures.

AI-Powered Drug Discovery Platform: Utilize artificial intelligence and machine learning algorithms to accelerate drug discovery processes and identify novel therapeutics.

Bioinformatics for Personalized Medicine: Develop a platform that analyzes genomic data to offer personalized treatment plans and preventive measures for various diseases.

Sustainable Biodegradable Packaging: Create biodegradable and eco-friendly packaging solutions to reduce plastic waste and its impact on the environment.

Next-Gen Plant-Based Meat Alternatives: Engineer plant-based proteins with realistic textures and flavors to offer environmentally friendly meat substitutes.

Nanotechnology-Enabled Drug Delivery: Design nanoparticles for targeted drug delivery to enhance treatment efficacy and minimize side effects.

Smart Agriculture Solutions: Integrate IoT devices and AI analytics to optimize crop yields, conserve resources, and ensure sustainable agriculture practices.

Microbiome-based Therapies: Develop therapies that leverage the human microbiome to treat various diseases and enhance overall health.

AI-Enhanced Mental Health Support: Create AI-powered chatbots and platforms to provide accessible and personalized mental health support and counseling.

Biofuel Production from Algae: Cultivate algae for biofuel production, a sustainable alternative to traditional fossil fuels.

Virtual Reality Medical Training: Develop virtual reality simulations for medical training and surgical practice to enhance skills and reduce training costs.

Genetically Engineered Bioluminescent Plants: Create glow-in-the-dark plants for decorative and functional lighting applications.

AI-Optimized Drug Combinations: Utilize AI algorithms to identify optimal drug combinations for synergistic therapeutic effects.

Personalized Nutrition Services: Offer personalized nutritional recommendations based on individuals' genetic and health data.

DNA Data Storage Solutions: Develop innovative methods for storing vast amounts of data using DNA as a medium.

Biofabrication of Human Organs: Use 3D bioprinting and tissue engineering to create functional human organs for transplantation.

AI-Driven Medical Image Analysis: Develop AI algorithms for accurate and rapid analysis of medical images, aiding in diagnosis and treatment planning.

Eco-friendly Biofertilizers: Create bio-based fertilizers that enhance soil health and crop productivity without harming the environment.

Non-Invasive Blood Glucose Monitoring: Develop wearable devices using advanced biosensors for continuous blood glucose monitoring in diabetic patients.

Bio-Inspired Renewable Energy: Design energy systems inspired by natural processes, such as mimicking photosynthesis to generate clean energy.

Telemedicine Platforms for Remote Areas: Create telemedicine platforms to provide healthcare access to remote and underserved communities.

Plant-Based Vaccines: Engineer plants to produce vaccine antigens, providing affordable and accessible immunization options.

AI-Enhanced Drug Repurposing: Use AI algorithms to identify existing drugs that can be repurposed for new therapeutic applications.

Edible Vaccines: Develop vaccines delivered through edible plant-based products, improving vaccination distribution and acceptance.

CRISPR-Based Disease Diagnosis: Utilize CRISPR technology for rapid and precise disease diagnosis at the molecular level.

Wearable Biosensors for Health Monitoring: Create wearable devices that continuously monitor vital signs and provide real-time health data.

Bioconversion of Waste into Bioplastics: Use microbes to convert organic waste into biodegradable bioplastics.

AI-Driven Drug Adherence Solutions: Develop AI-powered tools to monitor and improve patient adherence to medication regimens.

Environmental DNA Monitoring: Use environmental DNA sampling to assess and monitor biodiversity in ecosystems.

Precision Agriculture Drones: Develop drones equipped with sensors and AI to optimize farming practices and crop management.

Regenerative Medicine for Joint Repair: Use stem cells and tissue engineering for regenerative treatment of joint injuries and arthritis.

Microbial Enhanced Oil Recovery: Utilize engineered microbes to increase oil recovery from existing wells, reducing environmental impact.

AI-Powered Drug-Drug Interaction Prediction: Develop algorithms to predict potential drug interactions and adverse effects.

Customized Prosthetics with 3D Printing: Use 3D printing technology to create personalized prosthetics for individuals with limb loss.

Genetic Screening for Rare Diseases: Offer genetic screening tests to detect and diagnose rare genetic disorders early.

Blockchain-Based Medical Records: Create secure and decentralized platforms for storing and accessing patient medical records.

Biodegradable Implantable Medical Devices: Design medical implants that naturally degrade over time, reducing the need for additional surgeries.

AI-Enhanced Antibiotic Discovery: Utilize AI to identify new classes of antibiotics to combat antibiotic-resistant bacteria.

Microbial Fuel Cells: Develop microbial fuel cells that generate electricity from organic waste.

AI-Optimized Drug Dosage Formulations: Use AI algorithms to optimize drug dosage formulations for individual patient needs.

Environmental Biosensors for Pollution Detection: Create biosensors that detect and monitor environmental pollution and contaminants.

Therapeutic Microbiome Modulation: Develop therapies to restore and modulate the gut microbiome for various health benefits.

Smart Wearables for Elderly Care: Create wearable devices to monitor the health and safety of elderly individuals, providing remote care solutions.

Plant-Based Biopesticides: Engineer plants to produce natural compounds that act as biopesticides for agricultural pest control.

AI-Driven Drug Safety Prediction: Use AI to predict potential adverse drug reactions and improve drug safety.

3D Bioprinting of Skin for Wound Healing: Use 3D bioprinting to create skin substitutes for wound healing and burn treatment.

Blockchain-Based Clinical Trials: Implement blockchain technology to enhance transparency and security in clinical trial data.

Precision Medicine for Neurological Disorders: Develop personalized treatments for neurological conditions based on genetic and biomarker data.

Algal Bioremediation for Water Treatment: Utilize algae to remove pollutants and toxins from water sources.

AI-Powered Diagnostics for Infectious Diseases: Create AI algorithms for rapid and accurate diagnosis of infectious diseases.

Sustainable Textiles from Bio-Based Materials: Develop eco-friendly textiles made from bio-based sources, reducing the environmental impact of the fashion industry.

Please note that these startup ideas are purely fictional and meant for creative inspiration. As with any entrepreneurial venture, thorough research, market analysis, and domain expertise are crucial for the successful implementation of any startup idea.